"At Focus on the Family, we hear from couples every day who are struggling in their relationships and desperately seeking healing in their marriages. Through personal and pastoral experience—along with a keen understanding of biblical teaching—Chip Ingram casts a vision for marriage as God intends it. Better yet, he shows readers how to achieve the kind of marriage they've always dreamed of."

Jim Daly, president, Focus on the Family

"This is not just another book on marriage. Chip cuts through political correctness to get to the heart of Christlikeness by challenging both men and women to greater sacrifice in their relationship with one another."

Kyle Idleman, author, *not a fan.* and *Don't Give Up*

"If you are looking for a practical, biblically based picture of marriage, you need look no further. Chip Ingram has nailed it. I highly recommend *Marriage That Works*."

Gary D. Chapman, PhD, author, *The 5 Love Languages*

"A deeply life-giving marriage is not some elusive thing we strive for but can never achieve. To love God and love each other extravagantly is exactly what we were made for. Chip's wisdom and experience are evident on every page of *Marriage That Works*, and our marriages would look radically different if we let these truths change us."

Jennie Allen, author, *Nothing to Prove*; founder and visionary, IF:Gathering

"My friend Chip Ingram has provided couples with a practical, relevant tool to enhance their relationship to make it all that God intended it to be. You and your mate will be blessed as you live out the principles in this book."

Dr. Tony Evans, senior pastor, Oak Cliff Bible Fellowship; president, The Urban Alternative

"Chip Ingram writes from the uncompromising biblical foundation of God's design for marriage. His challenges for men and women are strong and yet sensitive, principled but practical. This book is a fresh approach to a continuing need. Each chapter has a set of study questions which will make this book very useful for personal or small group application."

Mark L. Bailey, president, Dallas Theological Seminary

"I quote Chip Ingram frequently. This is one of my favorite quotes of Chip's: 'Marriage is not a debate to be won; it is a dance to be enjoyed.' That's so true! In *Marriage That Works* Chip shows us how to enjoy the dance. His practical illustrations from his own marriage, coupled with the truth of God's Word, will help improve and transform your marriage."

Dave Stone, pastor, Southeast Christian Church, Louisville, KY

MARRIAGE
That
WORKS

GOD'S WAY OF BECOMING
SPIRITUAL SOUL MATES, BEST FRIENDS,
AND PASSIONATE LOVERS

CHIPINGRAM

BakerBooks

a division of Baker Publishing Group
Grand Rapids, Michigan

© 2019 by Chip Ingram

Published by Baker Books
a division of Baker Publishing Group
PO Box 6287, Grand Rapids, MI 49516-6287
www.bakerbooks.com

Printed in the United States of America

Library of Congress Cataloging-in-Publication Data
Names: Ingram, Chip, 1954– author.
Title: Marriage that works : God's way of becoming spiritual soul mates, best
    friends, and passionate lovers / Chip Ingram.
Description: Grand Rapids, MI : Baker Books, [2019] | Includes bibliographical
    references.
Identifiers: LCCN 2018028803| ISBN 9780801074554 (cloth)
Subjects: LCSH: Marriage—Religious aspects—Christianity. | Marriage—Biblical
    teaching. | Sex role—Religious aspects—Christianity. | Sex role—United States.
Classification: LCC BV835 .I54 2018 | DDC 248.8/44—dc23
LC record available at https://lccn.loc.gov/2018028803

ISBN 978-0-8010-7469-1 (ITPE)

19 20 21 22 23 24 25   7 6 5 4 3 2 1

In keeping with biblical principles of creation stewardship, Baker Publishing Group advocates the responsible use of our natural resources. As a member of the Green Press Initiative, our company uses recycled paper when possible. The text paper of this book is composed in part of post-consumer waste.

Contents

Introduction

O ne Thursday night, I got an overpowering whiff of Brut cologne as Dave, my mentor, came down the stairs. Dave had been trained by the Navigators and had launched two successful campus ministries in West Virginia. He was a blue-collar guy who laid bricks for a living, but whose passion was discipling college students.

Dave wore a big smile and a tie and sport coat—clothes I didn't even know he owned.

"What's going on?" I asked him. "Where are you going?"

"I'm going on a date." He grinned.

"With who?"

"Polly, of course. Who do you think?"

I was shocked. Dave and Polly had four kids—two in high school, one in middle school, and one in elementary school. I had never seen my or anyone else's parents go on a date unless they had to chaperone a dance. My folks loved each other, of course, but they did not look at each other the way Dave and Polly did even after twenty years of marriage.

I had been around Dave and Polly for about five years, moving with them to a new city after college graduation to help them launch a campus discipleship ministry. While Dave worked, I taught high school, coached basketball, and lived in the garage apartment behind Dave's house.

I had eaten more meals at their table than I can remember. I had seen their struggles. And I knew they really loved each other. But the picture of Dave coming down the stairs anticipating a date with his wife had an impact on me. It redefined what a marriage could be.

The Marriage God Wants for You

This book is about having that kind of marriage. Whether you and your mate are newlyweds or have been married for decades, God has designed this unique relationship to, over time, produce best friends, passionate lovers, and spiritual soul mates.

> *Best friends, passionate lovers, spiritual soul mates. That is the kind of marriage God wants for you and your mate.*

Best friends, passionate lovers, spiritual soul mates. That is the kind of marriage God wants for you and your mate. This is not hyperbole. It isn't idealism. It's a real possibility, regardless of where you and your spouse find yourselves.

Don't get me wrong. This isn't easy. It will require some *knowledge* that most people don't have, some *skills* everyone can learn, and a lot of *grace*, which God promises to provide.

It will also require setting aside some assumptions you've made about marriage, as well as mustering up the courage to honestly examine where your marriage is—and where you want it to be.

Paying a High Price

If you're thinking I'm one of those pastors from a long line of wonderful ministers who have had wonderful marriages and wonderful children—someone who has never had any problems, can't understand your marriage or your issues, and just wants to tell you how to do things the right way—you need to know that's not the case.

The kind of marriage I have with my wife is far better than I ever dreamed, but the price has been higher than I ever imagined. I don't mean to sound harsh about that; I'm just being honest.

Like many couples, Theresa and I carried a lot of baggage into our marriage. I came from a semifunctional alcoholic family, a background that is fairly common to those whose fathers served in World War II. Theresa's experience was even more severe, and it was complicated by an early marriage as an unbeliever to another unbeliever who found it more profitable to sell drugs than work—and more appealing to run off with another woman than to provide for his infant twin boys.

Theresa and I both came to know Christ in early adulthood, met a couple years after her husband left, were involved in a campus ministry in addition to having full-time jobs, were friends for about a year, dated for about a year, then married and left for seminary with two four-year-old boys. We had no premarital counseling and no money. I went to school full-time *and* worked full-time so she could care for the children. By God's grace, I adopted the boys a year later. Also by God's grace, one of my professors was Dr. Paul Meier, founder of the Meier Clinics, when less than a year into our marriage the wheels were falling off.

Theresa's and my journey has involved counseling, marriage exercises, reading books together, going to conferences, forgiving each other (again and again), learning to communicate, resolving anger, and figuring out how to get on the same page with money, values, in-laws, sex, parenting, and most of the big decisions of life, many of which we've disagreed on. Other than that, it has been pretty smooth!

Learning God's Design

How did we make it? I could tell you it was all by the grace of God, but as true as that is, it's too generic and not very helpful.

I could also tell you we got some very good insight from counselors and friends who helped us understand the issues from our pasts and our families of origin and who gave us some tools we needed to work on our marriage. That's true too, and I don't want to discount any of it.

But the fundamental reason we are still together and have the kind of marriage I always dreamed of—still with normal struggles like every couple has—is that we *learned God's design for the marriage relationship and committed to follow it.*

The Larger, Overarching Plan

This book is not a personal story, and I'm not a psychologist. I'm a pastor who has worked hard to have this kind of marriage and has spent thirty-five years counseling and observing Christians and non-Christians struggle, settle, and—far too often—quit.

The world doesn't need another marriage book that will give you psychological inventories, inspiring stories, and conventional advice. Plenty of those resources exist, and many of them are excellent. I have read, studied, and benefited from quite a few of them, both in my own marriage and in my ministry.

> *The world doesn't need another marriage book that will give you psychological inventories, inspiring stories, and conventional advice.*

What we do need in this day of sexual confusion, pop psychology, and addiction to narcissistic personal fulfillment is some very clear biblical truth from the Author of marriage—the One who created and designed it. And we need practical application of that truth.

God has communicated what marriage is, how it works, the roles and responsibilities for husbands and wives, and why his instructions are so important. He did this not only for the sake of marriage but also for his larger, overarching plan to reveal Christ's love to the world and his commitment to the church. That's why this book exists.

In the pages that follow, you will discover the power of making a covenant with your spouse. You will read some things that in today's culture may be considered politically incorrect. But they are foundational for a husband loving his wife well and taking responsibility for his God-given assignment. You'll read some challenging thoughts about how a wife must trust God and overcome fears of her husband's inadequacies.

Most of all, you will experience the beginnings of a spiritual, psychological, emotional, and physical oneness that you and your mate were both designed to enjoy.

With that in view, let's begin this journey together to discover God's design for the marriage you long to have.

1

God's Design for Marriage

Submit to one another out of reverence for Christ.

Wives, submit yourselves to your own husbands as you do to
the Lord. For the husband is the head of the wife as Christ is
the head of the church, his body, of which he is the Savior. Now
as the church submits to Christ, so also wives should submit
to their husbands in everything.

Husbands, love your wives, just as Christ loved the church
and gave himself up for her to make her holy, cleansing her
by the washing with water through the word, and to present
her to himself as a radiant church, without stain or wrinkle or
any other blemish, but holy and blameless. In this same way,
husbands ought to love their wives as their own bodies. He who
loves his wife loves himself. After all, no one ever hated their
own body, but they feed and care for their body, just as Christ
does the church—for we are members of his body.

"For this reason a man will leave his father and mother and
be united to his wife, and the two will become one flesh." This

is a profound mystery—but I am talking about Christ and the church. However, each one of you also must love his wife as he loves himself, and the wife must respect her husband.

—Ephesians 5:21–33

The early years of my marriage to Theresa were rocky, and there were times when I wanted to bail. But we stuck together and got professional help, and it was the best money we ever spent. Everyone has troubles; that's just part of marriage. What you do with them makes the difference.

Now, more than three decades later, we connect early in the day. We're early risers, and whoever gets up first makes the coffee. Maybe a half hour later, depending on the day, we talk about what's going on in each other's life, what the day looks like for each of us, what's coming up, where we're feeling pressure. It doesn't happen every day; sometimes one of us needs some alone time first. Often, I'll grab her hand and we'll talk to God together about what we're facing.

It took us some time, but we realized long ago that there is a design for this relationship. It works when we align ourselves with the design, prioritize each other's needs and fulfillment, and honor each other's uniqueness and relationship with God.

It's a lot like owning a high-performance car. You know it took years of planning, creating, and refining by the finest engineers and that it functions at its best only when you tune it to certain settings, use the highest-quality gas and oil, and are meticulous about maintenance. Marriage is like that.

The Master Designer of marriage has given us a manual for optimal performance. Marriage isn't easy to maintain, but neither is anything else that is valuable or worthwhile. His blueprint tells us how things work, and if we don't follow it, we will experience the consequences—as many in society are finding out nowadays. But unlike the instructions for high-performance machinery, these come from the loving heart of a Creator who wants his people to have deep, meaningful relationships with him and others. His Word tells us how.

One of the clearest pictures of marriage in Scripture is in Ephesians 5:21–33, and it works for every married person, even for those who are coming out of a dysfunctional past. It tells us about the role of a husband and a wife, how they should relate to each other, and what the higher meaning of their union actually signifies.

In this passage, Paul is writing to the Ephesians. He has just explained how they can be filled with the Holy Spirit and allow God to control their lives. He talks about the transformation in attitude that occurs when we are living by the Spirit's power. It's a beautiful and inspiring passage, but it begs a question or two: What does this spiritual life look like in real-life situations? How does it affect our relationships? Verse 21 begins with an explanation. Here's what a Spirit-filled marriage looks like. And it starts with a very unexpected statement: "Submit to one another out of reverence for Christ."

Words like "submission" are not received well in a culture that demands political correctness. They upset a lot of people. I can understand that, especially in light of the ways some of those concepts have been abused in the past. Whatever reservations you have about them, however, I want you to put them on hold for a bit.

We are going to explore what submission really means and the context in which it is to be lived out. I think you will find that the demands on each of us as marriage partners are equally challenging, stretching, and even impossible to accomplish in our own strength. God's instructions will not appear fair at first glance—until we realize the example he set for us and how the roles of husband and wife are both reflections of his extravagant love.

It Starts with Mutual Submission

There are three important initial observations about the Ephesians 5 passage, and being subject to one another is the first and foremost. Mutual submission is the only way a marriage can work.

First and foremost, each partner needs to understand that God is in charge of a marriage and that it should reflect his nature—his love, his concern, his radical sacrifice. It requires a selfless relationship because God is selfless. Marriage is not about fulfilling your own wants and needs; it's about fulfilling someone else's. If you enter into it thinking it's about you and getting your needs met, you're rejecting the design. Marriage is about honoring God and receiving from him whatever your spouse needs to get from him through

> *Mutual submission is the only way a marriage can work.*

you. That isn't easy. I understand that. But above all, it requires mutual submission to God and to each other.

Second, marriage won't work unless you learn how to love your mate not as you define love but as *God* defines it—and as your mate is designed to receive it.

As a husband, that means I am given an absolutely impossible job of loving my wife as sacrificially as Jesus loved the church—that I would actually give up my life for her, that I would nourish and cherish her and be sensitive to her needs. We husbands need to create an environment in which our wives will flourish. We can't do that on our own. We need divine help.

And wives are given the seemingly unreasonable commandment to do for their husbands what the church is to do for Christ: devote herself in service; partner with him in a degree of intimacy that stretches her level of trust; and respect him in ways that build him up, strengthen him to be the man he was created to be, and encourage him to do what he has been called to do. She can't do that without divine help either.

Third, this passage assures us that marriage has an even bigger purpose than our own happiness. Our joy, pleasure, and fulfillment are important to God, but they are only lasting within a larger context. According to this passage, marriage is a picture of an eternal relationship between Christ and the church. That is the blueprint behind the blueprint of marriage and family. God designed family to be a stable environment for offspring and a fundamental unit of society, yes. But it flows out of the eternal relationship designed for Christ and his bride, the church.

Demonstrating God through Your Relationship

One of the greatest opportunities you have to demonstrate the reality of God in your life is in your relationships, especially in how you get along with your marriage partner. In my experience the number one reason given for divorce is irreconcilable differences. In other words, "We just can't get along." People who do get along—who communicate well enough and compassionately enough to build each other up, even when they have differences—stand out.

Theresa and I once had a neighbor who got to see the good, the bad, and the ugly in our relationship because a next-door view provides that window into your life. Our kids and hers played together, we would occasionally talk in the yard, and sometimes we would invite her to church or to dinner. She was never very interested in spiritual conversations, but when she was getting ready to move, she said something I'll never forget.

"I've always been turned off by religion, and I'm not sure I believe in God, but over the years I've watched you and your wife. If I were ever going to be a Christian, I'd want to be one like you."

She was not saying that because she had seen a perfect marriage—not by a long shot. We made a lot of mistakes. But I think what she was trying to say was that she saw a man and a woman who loved each other through all of life's ups and downs. She saw commitment in a world that doesn't have many examples of it. And that made an impression about the kind of God we serve. In some way, our marriage was a reflection of the heart of the Master Designer.

God's Blueprint for Marriage

In the world of design and engineering, seeing a blueprint is necessary before you can implement a design. We can see the blueprint of marriage in the lives of those who are doing it as Scripture defines it. But an even simpler picture might help us envision how it works.

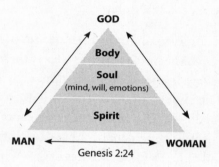

This equilateral triangle represents the basic premise of biblical marriage. God is at the top, of course. He created men and women in his image and designed us for the kind of relationship that embodies his nature and Christ's relationship with his people.

Marriage is his idea. That's really important to remember. Marriage is not just a social construct, one idea out of many others that developed in ages past as a good option for our society. No, it is written into the DNA of this world as God's normative pattern for the growth and development of humanity.

At the bottom of the triangle is a verse that points to the nature of marriage, established from the very beginning. Genesis 2:24 identifies the goal of marriage as oneness, or intimacy. "That is why a man leaves his father and mother and is united to his wife, and they become one flesh." When God created marriage, he said, "It is not good for the man to be alone" (Gen. 2:18). He designed it to address the problem of loneliness or isolation. A God of love by nature shares who he is; those made in his image are created to share themselves with someone else. The goal of marriage is for two beings—male and female—to be united as one, with hearts and minds and bodies that connect at every level.

From all I've observed about human nature over the years, that oneness is a basic human desire. Nearly three out of four Americans believe in the idea of a soul mate, according to a 2011 study. The largest group of true believers are under 30 (80 percent) or 30–44 (78 percent). The percentages drop for older folks, but still, 72 percent of those 45–59 and 65 percent of those 60 and older think soul mates exist.[1] Whether there's one Mr. Right or Mrs. Right for each person on earth is debatable. But there's no debating that we've been created to experience—and long for—an intimate, lifelong relationship.

Your Spiritual Connection Is the Foundation

Back to the triangle. Inside it, you will see three levels of connection—oneness in spirit, soul (mind, will, and emotions), and body. A biblical "soul mate" is fundamentally spiritual. It includes your relationship with God as well as your spouse's relationship with God. It is a triangle of unity, three spirits knit together in deep intimacy. The soul (mind, will, and emotions) and the body are certainly part of that. But the spiritual aspect is the biggest and most foundational part of what it means to be a soul mate.

There is a closeness in that process of growing in spiritual intimacy that ranks as high as sexual union. When spirits come together before God, he does something to draw a married couple together. It can be very awkward at the beginning, but later it's as natural as eating and breathing. Spiritual oneness with God and each other is meant to be the foundation of a marriage.

> *Spiritual oneness with God and each other is meant to be the foundation of a marriage.*

Sharing Your Soul: Your Mind, Will, and Emotions

In addition to spiritual oneness, God also wants us to have soul oneness. He wants you and your mate to be best friends.

Many married couples started out that way but are now just living as roommates; the mind, will, and emotional connections are not what they used to be. The goal was never for both of you to get absorbed in your jobs or for the husband to hang out with the guys all the time while the wife hangs out with her girlfriends. Too many couples spend their "together" time in the same room but with faces glued to a screen or a book. There's nothing wrong with reading or watching TV. But separate lives absorbed with separate activities undermine the connection, and it eventually goes away. That was never God's plan.

God wants soul mates to talk together, walk together, pursue hobbies together, and have some fun. Life will not always be just like it was when you were dating—that would be completely unrealistic. Many couples are disillusioned when the joy of dating fades away underneath the responsibilities of adulthood. But when you continue to date your spouse, it stirs those special feelings and excitement about being together—like my mentors you met in the introduction, Dave and Polly.

Soul oneness requires communicating and injecting some fun into the routines of your lives. Best friends support each other with the bonds of friendship—empathy, comfort, and affection. That kind of connection is at the heart of God's design for marriage.

The Bonding Power of Physical Union

As the icing on the cake, God designed physical oneness not only to fulfill the "be fruitful and multiply" (Gen. 1:28 NASB) command but also for our enjoyment. He wants married couples to be passionate lovers.

God designed men and women to bond in the sexual experience, not only physically but also emotionally and spiritually. The brain secretes the hormone oxytocin during and after sex, causing couples (especially men) to want to open up and share what's going on inside. The physical chemistry enhances the connection at every other level. God has wired that bonding into his creation and his design for marriage.

Historically, some Christian leaders have had trouble with the idea of passionate sex as a gift to married couples and have taught against it. Unfortunately, a consequence of that faulty teaching was to provide unhappy and unfulfilled people an "excuse" to seek physical fulfillment outside marriage.

Hebrews 13:4 tells us that God wants the marriage bed to be undefiled—sex is holy.

One of the biggest problems with society's perceptions of marriage is the separation of sex from the rest of the relationship so that people are led to believe that the best sex is outside of marriage. Ironically, secular studies have found that the best and most fulfilling sex in America is happening not in the singles scene or in extramarital affairs but in monogamous couples who are deeply committed to one another with high moral values.[2] I'm convinced from the way we are made that the physical relationship is meant to be the culmination of a foundational spiritual relationship and a mind-will-emotions relationship that flows out of the spiritual. Sex is the physical expression of a deeper union that serves its purpose only in the context of love and commitment.

Our culture has separated sex from love, which leaves people unfulfilled on both counts. Pornography, romantic fantasies, and illicit relationships are all examples of false intimacy that grow out of a society that does not understand the multiple connections of real intimacy. I recently read a statistic suggesting that more than two-thirds of people who get involved in extramarital affairs begin the relationship on social media.[3] If you're having struggles in your marriage and you connect online with an old flame from high school or college, it's easy to see where things might go from there.

I'm not suggesting that married couples delete their Facebook accounts or ignore old friends, but I am suggesting that we tend to treat our marriages too casually. And it isn't working out for us, is it? False intimacy in any area of life undermines unity in our homes, harms our children, can have devastating effects on our finances, and leaves us unfulfilled. It contradicts God's plan for our lives. He wants oneness for us at every level.

Closer to God, Closer to Each Other

I want you to try a little exercise with the triangle graphic.

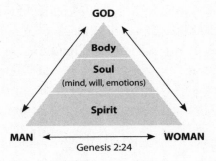

Put a finger on each of the corners that say "man" and "woman," and then slowly move your fingers up the sides to the point that says "God." Where are your fingers in relation to each other? They are closer, right? The point is simple, but it's also profound. The closer you grow to God, the closer you and your spouse grow to each other.

God designed marriage in such a way that it does not work as it should apart from him. It's true that many people who don't know him would say they are happily married, and I wouldn't argue with them. But are they as connected physically, emotionally, mentally, and spiritually as they could be? I don't think so.

And neither are many Christian couples. Just being a Christian doesn't change the dynamics very much. But I promise you that growing in intimacy with God changes everything despite our baggage and struggles. It was this passionate pursuit of Christ, which both Theresa and I were committed to, that saved our marriage. The greatest thing you can ever do for your marriage is to live as a committed, passionate follower of Jesus. You become like whomever you spend time with. When you spend time with God, he revolutionizes your heart and mind, and a new person shows up in your marriage. Only he can give you the power, freedom, and grace to give your mate what you could never give on your own.

> *The greatest thing you can ever do for your marriage is to live as a committed, passionate follower of Jesus.*

I married a selfish person. So did my wife. If you're married, there's a very good chance you married one too. All of us are innately self-centered until we mature. That's because of the sinful nature we inherited, and it can be remedied only by God's work in our lives.

The "satisfy me" urge in marriage never ends unless we make a radical decision to lay our own lives down, just as Jesus told his disciples to do. A husband lays down his life for his wife, and a wife comes under her husband to serve—not with the expectation that the other will respond but with the commitment to live sacrificially even if the other doesn't.

If that doesn't seem fair, it's because it isn't. But we aren't trying to work out what's fair, are we? We are trying to have a great marriage. And that's the only way to do it. That ends the cycle of selfishness and draws us close to God and to each other.

Spiritual Oneness, Deep Friendship, Physical Intimacy

After more than three decades of marriage, a lot of hard work, and plenty of struggles along the way, Theresa and I have found ourselves in a relationship in which we get what we need from each other because we are more focused on giving the other person what he or she needs rather than on seeking our own fulfillment.

I don't get up in the morning and read the Bible to cross an item off a list of spiritual requirements. I do it because I'm a desperate man in need of power and grace to give my wife what I would not otherwise be able to give her. She does the same for me. The result is a deep spiritual oneness, an ever-growing friendship flowing out of that, and then an intimate physical union that has produced a relationship beyond what words could ever express. That's God's design.

The blueprint for marriage as it is spelled out in Ephesians 5 tells us what marriage ought to look like. But underneath that blueprint is an even deeper truth about what marriage actually is. It is one thing to know what the blueprint is and another to know how to make it a reality in our lives. Ephesians 5 points us to the answers to that question of "how," and its truths may seem a little surprising, especially in today's world. But they are timeless truths that really work.

When we get a handle on these truths, we approach marriage in an entirely different way than our culture does, and we begin to discover and experience the crucial components of success.

――――――― **Questions for Reflection and Discussion** ―――――――

1. Why do you think most people identify a fulfilling marriage and family as something they want to experience in life? If this is such a strong desire, why do you think so few people are actually experiencing it?

2. Did you have realistic expectations when you first got married? Why or why not?

3. According to Ephesians 5, what does marriage illustrate? What bigger purpose does it serve?

4. Why doesn't being a Christian couple automatically imply having a better marriage? What must happen in any marriage—Christian or not—for a couple to grow closer to each other?

5. If you are married, which level of the relationship— spirit, soul, or body—has been the most fulfilling for you? List three things that originally attracted you to your spouse. Share those three things with your mate in a card or over coffee this week.

6. What one thing could you do this week to improve your marriage?

2

Is There a Man in the House?

Submit to one another out of reverence for Christ.

Wives, submit yourselves to your own husbands as you do to the Lord. **For the husband is the head of the wife as Christ is the head of the church, his body, of which he is the Savior.** Now as the church submits to Christ, so also wives should submit to their husbands in everything.

Husbands, love your wives, just as Christ loved the church and gave himself up for her to make her holy, cleansing her by the washing with water through the word, and to present her to himself as a radiant church, without stain or wrinkle or any other blemish, but holy and blameless. In this same way, husbands ought to love their wives as their own bodies. He who loves his wife loves himself. After all, no one ever hated their own body, but they feed and care for their body, just as Christ does the church—for we are members of his body.

"For this reason a man will leave his father and mother and be united to his wife, and the two will become one flesh." This is a profound mystery—but I am talking about Christ and the church. **However, each one of you also must love his wife as he loves himself, and the wife must respect her husband.**

—Ephesians 5:21–33

Little boys dream big. Ask them what they want to be when they grow up, and you'll get all kinds of fascinating answers: astronauts, presidents, athletes, superheroes, and even some pretty realistic professions that may or may not ever work out. If you ask them who they want to be like, they can come up with some big names—people who have made a name for themselves and an impression on their young audiences. And every once in a while, you hear one say something much more touching: "I want to be like my dad."

Those words come more easily for young boys than older ones. As boys grow into young men, the sentiment gets rarer. Perhaps their fathers have let them down, or maybe they've just seen a larger world of role models to choose from. Whatever the reason, of all the young men I have counseled or mentored over the years, only a few have ever pointed to their fathers as the men they most want to be like—as a Christian, a father, a husband, a man of integrity. It is an extremely high compliment that only a few men ever receive.

At a church I pastored, we had a gifted young staff team, and we often teamed up to teach the weekend services. Father's Day was coming up, so I casually asked around the room, "Who had a great relationship with their father?" Most of us on the team had major struggles with our fathers. There were eight of our key pastors in the room and each of them told their story. Out of that leadership team, there was not a single man in the room who could point to a positive relationship with his father. That's when I realized this is a really big deal.

Beginning with Mutual Submission

We are going to look at a picture of what a real man is, and we will see that genuine masculinity, as defined by God, does something life-changing in the people around us. It powerfully affects a man's wife, his children, and his friends. They become better people just by being with him. And it's never too late to become that kind of man.

Redefining manhood in marriage and in the home always begins with mutual submission. That's the umbrella concept covering the entire Ephesians 5 passage about relationships. Before Paul talks about the mystery of marriage and the roles of husbands and wives, he gives an instruction that precedes every other detail: "Submit to one another out of reverence for Christ" (Eph. 5:21).

This is really important. It provides the context for statements that trip people up when they read them in isolation.

The passages that follow Ephesians 5:21 explain roles not only for husbands and wives but also for parents and children and masters and servants (which we often apply today to the workplace). Whatever responsibilities and attitudes Christians are to have within all these relationships, the overarching attitude must be a sense of walking with God and putting other people first—expressing love and looking out for the best interests of others in all our relationships.

That alone should defuse a lot of the controversy surrounding the masculine and feminine roles Scripture describes for marriage. There are roles, but they are secondary to the context of mutual submission in the relationship.

The most important question, then, is not about who does what but about what mutual submission actually looks like. What does it really mean?

In the original Greek, the word "submit" that is used in this verse is *hupotasso*, and it is often used in a military context. It is a compound word: *hupo* meaning "under" and *tasso* meaning "to be in order or rank." It is the opposite of self-assertion. It urges subjection or submission to one another. Another way to think of it is a mutual desire to get less than one's due.

When both partners are engaging in mutual submission, it becomes a contest to see who can outdo the other in love and good works.

Think about what that means. What would it look like to be in a relationship with your mate in which, rather than each of you trying to get your way, each of you make it a goal to get less than your due in order to serve the other's interests? That's a different way to approach marriage than most people experience.

The issue is no longer which person is in control; the issue is which person is responsible. Mutual submission is the embodiment of a spiritual attitude that turns control over to God's Spirit and considers the person you are married to more important than you. If this sounds odd or even crazy to you as a man, I understand. God's design begins with him, and mutual submission to Christ and each other is where it all begins.

Learning the Dance

Mutual submission in marriage is like a dance floor. It is an open space where you have the freedom to move. It requires that the man and woman, each in a relationship with Christ as their Lord, come to each other not to take control but to serve. Each one asks, "How can I help you be successful? How can I express my love for you?" In this dance, the issue is not who takes the first step. It's the beauty of the movement itself.

Male chauvinism and female manipulation find no place on this dance floor. They have disappeared even before the first steps. Each person recognizes the importance of the other— this was never meant to be a solo act—and of the choreographer. They realize that every step honors the relationship and reflects well on the One who orchestrated it all.

If you have ever watched an elaborate dance routine, whether it was in a TV show like *Dancing with the Stars*, an ice-dancing competition, or a classic Fred Astaire and Ginger Rogers movie, you may have noticed that all the lifts and catches require a lot of trust. If the partners are not at the right place at exactly the right time, somebody could get hurt.

Dancers look at the dance differently than viewers do. Every step, every lift, every turn, every nuance has been choreographed ahead of time and rehearsed to perfection. They put in hours upon hours of work and years of preparation to create what appears to be a seamless piece of art.

Viewers, though, just see beauty and rhythm and flow. We don't have to know the discipline and technique behind all the steps and movements. We are looking at the whole.

That's like marriage. You have to know the choreography, you have to put a lot of practice into it, you have to trust—and the focus is not which person took the first step. You hear the rhythm of the music, see the movements, and try to absorb the beauty of it all. The attention is on the overall picture and how you move together as a unit.

An Ideal to Strive For

For the rest of this chapter, we will look at some of the ways men can make the dance more beautiful for their partners. In the book's following chapters, we'll also focus on how women do that too. But it all takes place on a dance floor of mutual submission, where, instead of being confining or restrictive, the divine "choreography" allows room for each partner to be at his or her most creative.

For the dance of marriage to be beautiful, God gives men and women different roles and movements. Those roles and movements have nothing to do with either partner being more important or whether the partners are equal. Rather, they have everything to do with function.

34

The man's role in the dance of marriage is as the one who leads. The bar is high for this role. For many men, it will take a lot of practice and retraining to step into it. But when you do, the woman in your life will feel loved, cherished, and completed. You will enable your family to move in the right direction at the right time for the right reason. Your children will grow up thinking you are the greatest man in the world, and they will have a healthy self-image and strong moral values. You will create a context for your loved ones to grow into their true selves as God designed them.

A word of warning, however. Sometimes a man's first reaction to this standard may be one of guilt. When I was taught the concept of true leadership early in our marriage, my response was, "Are you kidding? How could I ever possibly live up to this?"

> *God's instructions are meant to instill hope, not regret.*

That is not the intention here. God's instructions are meant to instill hope, not regret. The point is not to cover us with shame or give our wives yet another reason to tell us what we *should* be doing.

Instead, we're going to look at an image of true, God-designed masculinity for us to grow into. It is an ideal, not something for us to beat ourselves up over if we fall short. Rather, it is a clear target we should aim for and be fully committed to pursuing.

Choosing to Love Unconditionally

The marriage dance is described in Ephesians 5:22–33. You'll notice in that passage a role—"the husband is the head of the wife" (v. 23)—and a responsibility—"love your wives, just as Christ loved the church and gave himself up for her" (v. 25). You'll also notice that the word "love" comes up quite a few times. It is not the love of friendship (*phileo*), romance (*eros*), or family connection (*storge*). It is agape love. What's the significance of this?

Agape love is not, in its essence, an emotional love, though it may have emotions that come along with it. Agape love is choosing to give another person what they need the most when they deserve it the least, at great personal cost.

> Agape love is choosing to give another person what they need the most when they deserve it the least, at great personal cost.

Paul makes it clear that this is how Jesus loved us. When I was in sin, I didn't want God's help, and I certainly didn't deserve it, but Christ died in my place anyway. He did that to offer forgiveness and salvation to whoever would believe, allowing the Father to place our sin on him. Was any emotion involved in that sacrifice? Absolutely. We are told very clearly that Jesus did it "for the joy set before him" (Heb. 12:2), and he did it in spite of the agony that nearly overcame him as he prayed in the Garden of Gethsemane, "Not my will, but yours be done" (Luke 22:42).

Jesus's sacrifice was motivated by the kind of love that goes deeper than immediate feelings and is grounded in commitment and obedience to the Father's plan for our deliverance. This kind of love is a choice. That is the same kind of choice a husband is meant to make every day for his wife.

It is a wonderful thing when I treat my wife well, am sensitive to her needs, care for her, and respond to her in godly ways because I feel good about her. But if I do those things only when I feel good about her, we have a problem. I need to love her in the same way when she hurts me or acts in ways that distance me.

Agape love means giving her what she needs the most when she deserves it the least, at great personal cost. That isn't just hard to do. It's impossible—apart from the Spirit of God working in our hearts.

To Present Her in All Her Glory

Some might argue that Jesus's love for the church is different from a husband's love for his wife in some pretty significant ways. After all, according to the passage, Jesus gave himself up for the church in order to cleanse her and present her holy and blameless. A husband can't do that for his wife, can he?

If we demystify the language, "make holy" simply means "to set apart as special." A man can set his wife apart and honor her as special. Jesus did that for us, and the role of a man is to help his wife become the special person God intends for her to become. Jesus did it by the "washing with water through the word" (Eph. 5:26), the spoken word (*rhema*), speaking life into his church. A husband has the opportunity to speak life into the soul of his wife through affirmation and encouragement.

> A husband has the opportunity to speak life into the soul of his wife through affirmation and encouragement.

Ephesians 5:27 refers to Jesus presenting a "radiant" church to himself. Another Bible translation uses the phrase "in all her glory" (NASB). A husband is to make his wife radiant—to bring out the brilliance and glory that God has put within her. Nearly every woman has experienced some kind of rejection, and many struggle with deep insecurities about their real worth.

Theresa was rejected by her father and then her first husband. It amazed me how a beautiful woman like her could look in the mirror and see someone ugly. I learned early that my job as a husband is to help her see how beautiful she is, from the inside out, and how radiant, gifted, and valuable she is.

And I found that as I learned to love her and began to see her transform, she started responding in ways that met my deepest longings as a man. In loving her, I was actually doing something really good for myself.

No one is in a better position than a husband to help his wife overcome her sense of rejection by accepting her just as Jesus has accepted us. A man is to bring out the radiance and glory of his wife so she can be the woman God created her to be. It's been the most difficult but rewarding aspect of our marriage.

Nourishment That Grows a Marriage

A husband is commanded also to "feed and care for" his wife as Christ feeds and cares for the church (Eph. 5:29). Another word for this concept is "nourish." In the context of a relationship, it implies being devoted, providing for needs, and promoting the development and maintenance of health. A husband is created to develop, maintain, and help his wife—mentally, spiritually, emotionally, and relationally—become all that God created her to become. That's the kind of nourishment he provides.

This was a foreign concept to me when Theresa and I got married. I thought marriage meant being attracted to your mate, falling in love, making a commitment, having some kids, and letting things work out. I would play softball and basketball, help some with the kids, and hope everything would end up okay. That's all I knew. But as I grew as a Christian, I began to realize God had created my wife with one set of needs and created me with another set of needs, and we were created to be the instrument to meet each other's needs. We were designed for mutual nourishment. That's an entirely different approach to marriage. It has to be other-focused, a selfless expression of agape love.

The word for "care for" in this passage literally means "to keep warm." Relationally, it involves communicating in ways that make sense to each other. A husband is to give his wife a sense of safety and comfort.

When a woman says, "Let's talk," a caring response would be to open up and let her know what's going on inside. A lot of men don't understand the need in this area, and a woman probably won't explain it. Most women will begin a conversation not to fix a problem or share superficial information but to connect. She wants to know how her husband is feeling, what his fears and concerns are, and how he is processing them. She may want to pray together about what's going on inside. In contrast, men typically want to exchange information, get something done, and have conversations that have a transparent purpose and solve problems.

Navigating Our Insecurities

Remember the bigger picture here. A woman is looking for a man who will assume the same kind of responsibility for his wife that Jesus demonstrated for the church, even to the point of sacrificing himself for her. She wants a man who embraces his devotion to her by nourishing and cherishing her, a man who sees his God-given role as provider not only for her external needs but also for her heart. That's a real man from God's perspective.

Most of us men never saw that as we were growing up. Our role models taught us that real men make a lot of money, play hard, live their own lives, and maintain their marriages by taking care of their wives' external needs. A few men have seen great examples of biblical manhood up close, but most of us have had to piece together this picture of real masculinity as we have grown and learned what Scripture says. It can seem so far over our heads that we may wonder if we can ever pull it off. But if we ask God to help us be that kind of man, regardless of which stage of life we are in, he will answer. And when he does, some fantastic things begin to happen in our relationships.

One of the reasons we men have difficulty being successful leaders in our homes is that we can be very insecure about our role there. We don't always come across that way, but beneath the surface, we struggle with how to care for a woman's heart. Many of us do not navigate the inner world very easily because whenever we encounter a problem, we want to fix it, and some of the deep inner workings of the human heart are not quick fixes.

Sometimes that isn't even the goal; women often want to have a conversation not for the purpose of problem solving but just to be heard. We don't always know what to do with that. We know how to do our jobs, shoot a basketball, and fix a faucet. We're comfortable in those worlds. But to help our daughters grow in their femininity? Discipline a child with sensitivity to whatever is going on inside him? Pray with our wives? Those are different matters. They pull us into areas where we are unskilled, untrained, and most insecure.

But it doesn't have to stay that way. As we learn to make these things our priorities and get to know God and understand how he has designed us to serve our wives and families, real change happens.

Five Diagnostic Questions

Answering these questions will tell you who is leading your home.

Again, the purpose of these questions is not to induce guilt. It is to make you aware.

In the first two years of our marriage, my answers to most of these questions would have suggested that Theresa was the leader in our home. I needed to become aware of my lack of leadership and by God's grace take responsibility.

That's the point of this exercise—awareness that leads to change through a process of growth and grace. Read the following questions with that purpose in mind.

1. **Who initiates spiritual growth in your home?**

   Who says, "Let's sit down and talk about this. Let's see what the Bible says about it. Maybe we need to spend some time praying about it"?

2. **Who handles the money?**

   This question is not about who makes the most money; that isn't the issue at all. Some wives make more than their husbands, and that is no indication of who is exercising leadership in the marriage. But which one of you is assuming the responsibility for making sure bills get paid on time? If the wife is managing money and writing checks, is she doing that as a function of her gifts or because her husband is neglecting his responsibility and leaving it to her?

3. **Who disciplines the children when you are both at home?**

   Each parent will need to discipline a child at various times and in different situations, but when the problem behavior is relevant to both spouses and you are both present to deal with it, which one of you takes the lead?

4. **Who initiates talking about problems, future plans, and areas to develop?**

   For example, how do you decide how many kids you want to have? What school they should go to? What kind of jobs you and your spouse should take? When you should retire? What the course of your life together will look like?

5. **Who asks the most questions in your home, and who gives the most statements?**

   Who is the one who is always asking what to do for dinner or about the decision you need to make about next week's plans? Whichever person is asking those questions is the one who feels the weight of responsibility for them.

None of these questions are meant to prompt a legalistic standard in your marriage. Women will often see issues that men don't see, so they will naturally be the ones to bring them up first. There's nothing wrong with that. Many women are gifted with making plans and orchestrating schedules in ways that their husbands are not, so it is perfectly normal for them to contribute their gifts in those areas.

The real question is, Who is carrying the weight of responsibility in the marriage? Many women have to initiate discussion, make plans, and ask the big questions because their husbands do not. These men don't want to shoulder the responsibility for making life work. They let their wives carry the burden. When this happens, wives do not feel cherished, nurtured, and protected. In other words, they are not getting what God designed for their husbands to give them.

That is what these diagnostic questions are getting at, and if they reveal a pattern of neglect, some of the dynamics in the relationship need to change.

How to Love Your Wife: Step Up

Let's get down to the nitty-gritty. Ephesians 5:33 calls men to love their wives as they love themselves. How do you do that? As a man, how do you get out of unhealthy patterns to free your wife's heart from the burdens you were meant to carry? How do you grow deeper into true manhood? If marriage is a beautiful dance, a man needs to step up—in leadership and in love.

You might hear the same language from a coach anytime the star player goes down with an injury. Everyone else on the team will just need to "step up." That is a great way to express God's design for a man in his marriage and his family relationships. We men need to step up in leadership and step up in love in order to fulfill our God-given role.

If marriage is a beautiful dance, a man needs to step up—in leadership and in love.

I believe there are three specific ways to love your wife the Ephesians 5 way that will change the nature of your relationship: (1) love her sacrificially, (2) love her intentionally, and (3) love her sensitively.

Love Her Sacrificially

Paul's instruction to husbands to love their wives sacrificially is clear from Ephesians 5:25. The kind of love Jesus has for the church cost him something. The kind of love a husband has for his wife should cost him something too.

One of the ways you can love your wife sacrificially is in how you demonstrate your preferences. When you choose her over the other "loves" in your life, you make a statement about her value to you.

Years ago when our kids were young, I was just learning about how marriage is supposed to work. I was watching the Slam Dunk Contest of the NBA All-Star Game, and my boys and I were rooting for the players and screaming at the acrobatic dunks. These were some of the greatest players in the game, and I had been waiting all year to watch this. But I happened to look over at Theresa across the room, and she wasn't mad or upset—there was nothing disapproving about her countenance at all—but I got the feeling that not everything was right in her world. Something was bothering her.

I had a thought that could have only come from God, because I never would have thought it myself. A voice inside my head said, "Chip, why don't you get up and ask Theresa if she wants to go on a walk. Find out what's going on inside." My first reaction was to push that thought aside. We could take a walk anytime—the contest was going on right then. But I usually don't have promptings like that, and this one was persistent.

So, amid the bewildered looks of my sons, I walked over and asked her how she was doing. She said she was fine and told me to go ahead and watch the game, but I could tell something was still not right. I told her I would catch it later on a replay. So we went for a walk.

She started opening up, and I realized there was a lot going on inside her. We ended up getting a cup of coffee afterward and talked a little bit more. Going on a walk with Theresa wasn't a huge sacrifice, but she turned to me and said, "Chip, I feel so loved right now."

"Why? I didn't do anything." We had just walked around, I asked a few questions, but mostly I listened for about an hour. Like most men do, I was thinking we hadn't really accomplished anything. No problems got fixed.

"I know how much you love sports. And for you to leave that behind to talk to me really sent a powerful message," she said.

I had made a choice—not even a very big one, in the grand scheme of things—that reflected my preference for her over other things going on in my life. It wasn't a huge sacrifice, but it meant something to her. It made a statement about her value to me.

Before we go on, what would that statement look like in your life this week? What small sacrifice would say to your wife that she matters more than that "something else" in your life?

Another way to love your wife sacrificially is to invest time in her. A lot of men work long hours during the week, and on their one day off, they spend five or six hours on the golf course or pursuing some other hobby independently of the family. If this describes you, not only does that leave your

45

wife with very little of your time, but one day when your kids are grown, you'll want a lot of those hours back, and you won't be able to get them. Your golf game will be a little better, but your children will grow up with some emotional voids in their hearts. That is not a good trade-off.

You do need to have hobbies, to connect with other men, and to get some exercise. Those things are important for a balanced life. But to step up as a leader in your home and to love your wife sacrificially, you will need to adjust your priorities and invest your time in her and your children.

It took me some time to learn how to do this, and I wasn't good at it initially. But we developed a habit in our family of eating dinner together at 5:30 five or six nights a week. I was leading a large church, and I certainly had demands on my schedule before and after that time, but my family knew I would be there at 5:30 to eat with them. After eating, we would push our plates to the middle of the table and just talk. We laughed, joked, talked about school and friends, and communicated what we were hearing from God and the challenges we were experiencing. Sometimes we would pray together, other times we would read a passage, or we would simply talk.

Then, at least a couple nights a week, I would take over the kids' bath time and tuck them into bed. I didn't want Theresa to get all the fun in connecting with them. That requires time, but believe me, it's worth it. Your wife and your children will treasure your investment in them.

For most of the years of our marriage, I have had a weekly date with Theresa. Since I had never seen a married couple have a date when I was growing up, it was a foreign concept to me, but it was one way I could show her she was important to me. So every Friday, my day off, we went to breakfast together. For three or four hours, she knew we were going to hang out together. And those times shaped our marriage.

We have read books and listened to CDs and discussed them together. I didn't know what I was doing as a father and husband, and she was learning how to be a wife and mother, but we realized a lot of people had gone before us and learned some good lessons about marriage and family. So we would read their books or listen to them and try out whatever might work for us. Theresa was very cooperative and encouraging; she had a lot of patience toward me. And over time,

> *Your wife and your children will treasure your investment in them.*

we have grown in more ways than I could have imagined. But it takes time, and it costs something. It requires sacrificial love.

Another cost of sacrificial love is rejection. When we come out of denial and deal with some of the problem areas in the home—a rebellious child or a harmful behavior pattern—it causes some friction. Sometimes the kids don't want to sit down and have a meal together. You can be passive and let them do what they want to do or you can take the lead and say, "Here's what we're doing." And you just might experience some rejection. A father who intentionally leads his family has to be able to handle that.

Leaders change things, and not everyone likes the change. Some people prefer the status quo. Sometimes the kids will take a smart-aleck tone and say, "Who do you think you are? You don't run my life." And if it really escalates, you will have to impose discipline, which is never fun for anyone involved. The stakes get higher as the kids grow older. It goes from "time-out" to "hand over your car keys" faster than you ever thought it would. But as a leader and a parent, you do have control.

I'm always amazed at fathers who say they don't have any control over their children. "They just go to their room, slam the door, and play video games." But whose house are they living in? Whose food are they eating? Whose cars are they driving? A short-term loss of privileges is far better than a long-term lack of discipline or character. And some kids, even though they will never show it, are desperately hoping for someone to place boundaries around them and demonstrate the love of discipline. Women may have a harder time expressing that kind of authority, especially with adolescent boys—that's one reason so many boys have big problems when there isn't a man in the house—but your manhood gene was given for both the soft and hard sides of fatherly love. Enduring the rejection that comes with fulfilling your responsibility in the home is not easy, but it is worthwhile. Your kids will eventually come back to you and say, "Thanks, Dad." And they will grow up to become that kind of parent too. Sacrificial love endures the cost of the moment for the sake of the big picture.

> *Sacrificial love endures the cost of the moment for the sake of the big picture.*

Love Her Intentionally

Ephesians 5:26–28 tells us that Jesus had a plan for his church. He purposefully sanctified her, cleansed her, and sought the best for her. You will need to do the same for your wife.

Have you ever asked her what her dreams are? What spiritual gifts God has given her and how she wants to use them in this season of life? How you can help her do what she feels like God created her to do? You are not only her leader; you are also her facilitator. God has given her to you to help support you in your God-given mission in life, but loving her sacrificially means doing the same for her. One of your greatest opportunities in marriage is to purposely seek to develop your wife's beauty and gifts and to help her grow spiritually, emotionally, and physically.

Imagine your wife as a flower. You can't make her grow and bloom, but you can create the right conditions for her to do so. You can be an instrument in the hands of God to help her grow into the beauty she was created to display. To do that, you will need to be her number one cheerleader and encourager, to recognize gifts in her that she doesn't even see, and to call out the treasures that God has placed inside her. Though only God can cause growth, you have a huge role in creating the right environment.

Soon after we got married, Theresa wrote our first Christmas letter to friends and family. I had been writing all kinds of papers in seminary, but I read her letter and thought, *She writes so much better than I do.* I told her so. "You're just saying that because you're my husband," she replied. I had to work to convince her because, as many women do, she minimized her gifts.

Later, I heard her explaining something to someone, and I thought, *Wow, she really communicates well.* And, of course, she denied it. But in our first church, a group of about a dozen ladies asked her to speak. Theresa didn't think she could do it, so I encouraged her. We went over her outline together. It was a little terrifying for her, and she felt sick for days before the event, but she just needed someone to believe in her. She needed someone to say, as often as necessary, "You can do this. You have a gift for it."

Twenty years later, she taught a series called "Precious in His Sight" at a women's retreat, and it helped women so much that we made it part of the *Living on the Edge* radio broadcast. People loved it. Her series actually had a greater response than mine. Some husbands might feel threatened by that, but I remembered all the years of dreaming that Theresa would grow into her gifts and that God would use them. She was blooming in ways I had always wanted to see her bloom.

I remember when Theresa was entering into the early part of midlife and thinking of all the health issues that can affect women as they get older. She wanted to be proactive about them. But she had no athletic background. I love working out—I would do it twice a day if I could and it would not feel like a discipline—but Theresa didn't even know where to begin. She mentioned her concerns when we were on vacation one year, so I suggested we start walking together. We've been walking ever since, and some of the best times of our marriage have come out of the conversations we have had on those walks.

Theresa also mentioned how she had always been intimidated by gyms. So I rearranged my schedule for two years so that during my lunch hour on Mondays, Wednesdays, and Fridays we could work out together and I could show her how to use the machines and lift weights. It made a huge difference to her. It was a sacrifice, but a small one in light of the payoff. When you love your wife intentionally, the benefits always far outweigh the costs.

This never ends. You will always be in a position to help your wife develop into the person God created her to be. Loving your wife intentionally is a big job, but you will never regret it. She will grow spiritually, emotionally, physically, relationally, and in every other way as you encourage her and help her see what she may not have seen in herself.

Love Her Sensitively

Little things can be big things for women. As you nourish and cherish her, don't always look for the big gestures.

Little words of encouragement make a huge difference. Calling when you have no reason to call touches her in a way most men will not understand. Planning a date and working out all the arrangements makes her feel secure and loved. Noticing what needs to be fixed around the house, the stresses you can relieve for her, and the plans that need to be made will make her life a little bit easier and her heart a lot fuller.

It's what many women call "sensitivity." It means being aware of what's going on in her life and being willing to meet her there.

I have a set of faded index cards that I have had since the early '80s. I had been married about four years, and I was learning many of the principles in this book. But they weren't sticking. I would be a good husband for about a week, then default back to the habits and patterns I had developed growing up. So I decided to write down on these index cards the kind of husband I wanted to be, thinking that if I read them over and over again each day, eventually my new identity as a husband would stick.

It's a little embarrassing to read them now, but my "Life Goals with Wife" look like this:

- *My goal is to love Theresa sacrificially in a way that makes sense to her.*

  I wanted to remember what my job was, so that was number one.

- *My goal is to be the leader and initiator in our family that God wants me to be.*

  I had not seen that modeled for me as I was growing up, but I wanted to be different.

- *My goal is to get away with Theresa alone three times each year.*

  I don't think I ever accomplished that when we had young children, but we usually got away at least twice. Compared to before—which was "never"—that was a huge improvement.

- *My goal is to make our home a beautiful place to live, within our priorities financially, as a gift to Theresa.*

I didn't notice a lot of things she noticed. We had an old dishwasher that leaked water, so she would always have to put towels underneath it. Our kids' rooms had old windows, so she put towels under them to absorb the rain when it came in. She would tell me about these things, and I would just think of how much money a dishwasher and new windows would cost. Towels seemed like a pretty good option. But I realized that our home was her domain, the environment she spent most of her time in. That's the place God designed her to oversee. I needed to cooperate with him. So without being extravagant and living beyond our means, I learned to do whatever I could to create a good environment for her to live and work in.

- *My goal is to read with Theresa once a week.*

That did not work every week, but we have read dozens of books together in the years since I wrote that goal.

- *My goal is to pray seriously with my wife once a week and briefly each day.*

That doesn't sound like a big deal, especially for a pastor. But when I've spoken at pastors' conferences, I've asked how many do this, and very few hands go up. It doesn't happen if it is not intentional.

- *My goal is to give my wife what she needs instead of what she wants.*

As a leader, you need to do what is best. One of the dangers is to think that a loving husband will say yes to whatever his wife wants, but that can produce codependency. Your goal is to do what is best for her, for your marriage, and for your family. At times, that will mean saying no to something because you can't afford it or you don't see it fitting into long-term goals. You might experience some conflict and rejection over that. But showing up as a man in the relationship has a powerful effect that is good for you, her, and the family as a whole.

What Loving Sacrificially Does *Not* Mean

After about a year and a half of trying to fulfill all of Theresa's desires, I read a book on codependency and realized that it described me perfectly. I needed to make some adjustments.

Being a loving husband does not mean giving your wife whatever she wants or satisfying her every desire. Ultimately, God is the fulfiller and satisfier. A husband creates the conditions that give God room to work. As a man, you will often be God's instrument in her life, but you won't be everything for her.

Loving her sacrificially also does not mean that you can never have a life of your own. You need male friends, hobbies, and time to be alone. You need to plan some times to get with other men, have fun, and be refreshed. Your wife will need to understand your need for healthy activities alone and with other men and cooperate with that so you can bring your best self to her.

But this needs to be balanced. Some men will spend much more time cultivating a world of their own and then entering the worlds of their wives and children only occasionally. You need to be able to find a balance and do both.

Loving your wife sacrificially also does not mean that you make her dependent on you. She needs to have her own self-identity too. Sometimes you will take care of things for her; at other times, you will encourage her to do things on her own. You don't want to smother her; you want her to grow.

Theresa came from a town of about two hundred people, so when we first moved to Dallas, she didn't know what to do with six lanes of traffic. I would always drive whenever we had to go downtown. But I realized this was reinforcing her dependence on me, and it was really limiting her. She had to call me every time she needed to take one of the kids to a doctor's appointment downtown. So despite her early objections, I made sure she got behind the wheel and grew in confidence with cars zipping in and out and around her. Pretty soon she could drive anywhere because she overcame her fears. Sometimes we need to give our wives room to grow and express by our behavior that we have confidence in them.

Many men will recognize a potential no-win situation here. If you do a lot of those things for her, she may accuse you of believing she can't do anything for herself. If you back off of some of the things she wants you to do and leave them for her, she may get upset because you won't help her out.

That dynamic prompted another index card: "Father, give me the wisdom to know how to give my wife what she needs, not what she wants, so that I love her the way you love her."

I had to get to a point where I realized not all conflict is bad. It can help both spouses grow. But the goal is always to empower our wives, not to avoid responsibility. We have to learn the difference.

Finally, *loving sacrificially does not mean calling all the shots*. That is not biblical manhood. It means you talk together, you pray together, you get God's counsel together, you work as a team, and at the end of the day, you do what you're called to do. You lead so you can dance together, not so you can be the featured performer.

Meant to Make a Difference

Unfortunately, many husbands are living in a way that is slowly killing them. You were made to lead, to be strong, to have courage, and to make a difference. Somewhere between the false extremes of dominance and negligence is a kind of leadership and responsibility that involves sacrifice and sensitivity. You were made to feel the responsibility and joy of watching your partner bloom and develop and, if you have children, to watch them bloom and develop too. You matter, you are valuable, and you can do this by the grace of God.

You will notice that your efforts to love your wife sacrificially are not only personally challenging and will require you to overcome some past habits and attitudes. Your efforts will also be challenged by a culture that does not embrace these values or give you many good examples of how to live them out.

There are reasons so many men have to learn what it means to be the kind of husband God calls them to be. We will explore some of those challenges and how to overcome them in the next chapter.

—————— **Questions for Reflection and Discussion** ——————

1. What are some of the pitfalls and misunderstandings of the word "submission" in biblical descriptions of marriage? How does the idea of mutual submission address these misunderstandings?

2. Why is the metaphor of dance such an effective picture of marriage? What elements of a dance do you think help clarify the roles of men and women most?

3. Why is clarity of roles important in marriage? What happens when marriage partners are not clear about each of their roles?

4. If you are a man, which aspects of sacrificial love seem most challenging to you? If you are married, what immediate practical steps can you take to love your wife more sacrificially, intentionally, or sensitively?

5. If you are a woman, what attitudes and actions do you think will most help the man in your life grow into his role as the Bible defines it?

3

The Evolution of the American Man

I f you feel overwhelmed, maybe even downright inadequate, after reading the last chapter, welcome to the club. Everything in that chapter was completely foreign to me before I got married. In fact, it was foreign to me in the early years of our marriage, as evidenced by the need for counseling and the deep struggles and dissatisfaction we both had, despite loving each other deeply.

You may feel as if the ideals presented here only give your mate more ammunition to point out where you don't measure up, but that's not what this book is about. And it certainly isn't about pouring more guilt on the secret wounds that most of our wives have no idea we carry. The chapters for men are for guys like you and me who really want a great marriage but don't know exactly what that looks like and how to make it happen. So let's review and tackle this God-sized assignment with his power and grace.

In the last chapter, we learned that God has called us men to *step up* and give our lives to lead and love our wives and families in the context of Christlike mutual submission. I outlined three things that God commands husbands to do:

- We must love our wives *sacrificially*.

- We must love our wives *intentionally*.

- We must love our wives *sensitively*.

What husband doesn't want to be this kind of man? But why is it so hard?

Why is this model of biblical leadership within marriage such a different paradigm from what most of us saw in our own homes growing up?

What forces today are working against us as we try to become that kind of man and that kind of husband?

And, most importantly, how do we break the habits learned in the past to become the men we long to be, the husbands our wives need us to be, and the models our children are desperate to see?

I want to take you on a journey that will help you understand the problem, perhaps like never before. I want you to understand how and why the depiction of manhood has changed drastically in the last five or six decades. I call it the evolution of the American male. It's why we don't know what it looks like to step up as men.

The Evolution of the American Male

Perceptions of expectations for men and women, and marriage, have changed more in the last fifty to sixty years than in the previous two thousand. Those of you who have lived fewer than, say, four decades have grown up entirely inside the dynamic of today's culture. You may not realize how all of today's television, movies, books, social media, and marketing messages are opposed to the God-given design for marriage.

That's a dramatic statement, isn't it? We need to understand where we came from and how we got here to see the direction of our culture and thus be able to push back and live biblically.

Trends since at least World War II have eroded the concept of manhood—with devastating consequences.

In the early 1950s, American soldiers had recently come home from World War II, the "baby boom" was expanding families, suburbs were flourishing, and the vast majority of young boys and girls had both a father and a mother in the home. They were building the American dream. Divorce wasn't unheard of—movie stars were getting them, and occasionally it would happen to someone closer to home—but for the most part, it was a rare occurrence. That doesn't mean every couple was happy, but they usually weren't looking for overt, legal ways out of the marriage. The family unit was a pretty stable anchor for society.

That changed in the '60s. The Vietnam War and widespread restlessness over issues of race and justice combined to cause people to question all social norms, including sexual morality. For many people, existentialism became not just a European philosophy but an American way of life. Truth became relative. Authority (of any sort) deserved to be questioned, undermined, ignored, or destroyed.

The rallying cry was "Make love, not war." Sex, love, and marriage became separate categories. They no longer had to go together. Sex did not imply any commitment of love and certainly not of marriage. Men could openly be biological fathers without embracing any responsibilities of fatherhood. The stability of the family began to disintegrate.

The radical feminism of the late '60s and '70s went well beyond the important issue of getting equal pay for equal work. It not only aimed to put men and women on equal footing, but it also aimed to erase any differences in standards for the way men and women behave and the roles they have in society. It denied differences to the point of emasculating men.

By the 1980s, people began to tire of sexual issues and focused on themselves: the "me" decade. The emphasis on affluence and greed—living as if the goal in life were to acquire more and more—naturally led to an epidemic of workaholism. Many fathers (and mothers) turned their attention away from their families to focus on careers. Many single-income families turned into two-income families, as rising costs and changing work dynamics stretched family expenses beyond past income levels.

By the 1990s, society was no longer grounded in any coherent understanding of family norms. Confusion disoriented an entire generation. Sex roles were blurred, open homosexuality increased, the family unit was redefined, and the culture began to normalize behaviors that were once considered marginal. By the 2000s, "diversity" had become the only "norm" that anyone could identify as a consistent standard for families.

The effects on children of fathers being absent from the home are staggering. In America, 23.6 percent of children (24 million) lived in father-absent homes in 2016,[1] and 63 percent of youth suicides are from fatherless homes.[2] Children living in fatherless homes have a poverty rate of 47.6 percent, over four times the poverty rate of children living in married-couple families.[3]

Many people will never have a clear understanding of why marriage is even desirable. If it doesn't work, why keep doing it? The majority of young couples live together before they get married, if they ever do, which actually undermines the marriage before it ever starts. The emotional fallout in this generation is not hard to see.

To be fair, much of the social change that has come since the 1950s has been positive. Social expectations sixty years ago pushed many people into conventional careers and family situations that were not fulfilling or suited to their gifts or interests. Women were rarely treated equally or even taken seriously. The "normal" roles people played were often a veneer covering a much more complex reality. My parents and Theresa's were "doing family" right in the middle of that generation, and clearly, they were wrestling with some pretty serious issues. Not everything was rosy.

But the positive changes have come at a significant cost and with a lot of negative baggage. Those of us who have been around for a while have seen the fracture and fragmentation of an entire culture, with numerous damaging side effects.

Dumbing Down Dads in the Media

If you want a visual picture of how society has changed and how our perceptions of manhood have been redefined, look at the iconic TV fathers over the last few decades. If you're much younger than I am, you may not remember Ward Cleaver, although you may have come across reruns of *Leave It to Beaver* (1957–63). Mr. Cleaver had a good job, provided and cared for his family, and was always there for paternal discipline and wise guidance if Beaver or Wally ever got into trouble (which they did, every episode). He was the voice of reason and an anchor for his family. If you're even older than I am, you might recall earlier popular shows like *The Adventures of Ozzie and Harriet* (1952–66) and *Father Knows Best* (1954–60).

The next generation of TV introduced us to *The Brady Bunch* (1969–74), where the father handled a blended family of six kids in partnership with his wife, but still with the kind of paternal wisdom portrayed in traditional father roles. Then in the late '70s and into the '80s, things began to change.

We saw a movement away from family units in entertainment: *Three's Company* (1976–84) pushed the boundaries of television standards and played with expected gender roles. *Murphy Brown* (1988–98) represented feminism at its peak, as the lead character managed to have her career and be a single mother without any need or desire for a man in her life. In the '90s, *Friends* (1994–2004) showed us what an extended adolescence looks like—how to sleep with whomever you wanted to sleep with and move in and out of marriages as needed. And don't even get me started about the dysfunctional *Married with Children* (1986–97), which presented the antithesis of a real man and a godly marriage.

The Simpsons (launched in 1989) has shown us the absolute lowest point of fatherhood in Homer Simpson, a bumbling, know-nothing fool who earns plenty of laughs and no respect. He may be an extreme example, but if you think through all the family sitcoms that have been produced in the last couple of decades, you'll find very few examples of strong manhood and quite a few examples of husbands and fathers who are either tolerated or beloved for their quirks while their wives really run the family.

You would be hard-pressed to find a representation of a strong, compassionate, sensitive, courageous, providing, protective man in recent TV shows or movies. The days of *Father Knows Best* and *Leave It to Beaver* are gone.

We know, of course, that those shows were idealized pictures of family life; few families in the '50s and '60s actually functioned like that. But the ideals of an age are significant. They demonstrate how Americans wanted to perceive the role of the man at home, and those desires and expectations have almost completely deteriorated over the years.

In addition to television and film role models, our heroes have changed. They are no longer warriors or strongman characters (which, admittedly, were sometimes over the top);

they are athletes and entertainers, whether actors or singers. There's nothing wrong with appreciating what celebrities do, but competing and entertaining are jobs, not courageous acts of manhood. Actors pretend to be other people. Singers and musicians make music. Athletes play. They get a lot of money too, and many of them are incredibly talented. But their accomplishments have little to do with character and integrity, as we have seen again and again.

Unfortunately, though, they're our children's role models. A young boy used to say he wanted to be a fireman or policeman or even the president. Now it's more likely to be an NBA player or a rock star. What does that mean for how the next generation views manhood?

Absent-Father Families

We live in a culture that devalues true manhood and marriage. One of the consequences is families without fathers or those whose fathers are passive.

I dated a girl in high school and went over to her house one day to meet her mother. After the usual small talk, I noticed a picture on the mantel of a man in a military uniform. He was a good-looking guy with a nice smile on his face. I asked who he was, and my friend said, "That's my dad."

"Oh, is he around?" As soon as I asked, my friend's face fell and the room got quiet.

Her mother filled in the story. "Her father has been missing in action in Vietnam for a number of years now. We don't know if he's alive or dead. We pray every single day that he'll come back home one day, but we don't know. We just wait."

That had to be an incredibly difficult situation, through no fault of my friend or her mother. Nobody had made bad decisions to break up this family. But the effects were just the same. It became apparent as I got to know them that there were some real deficits in their lives—a girl growing up without experiencing her father's love, a woman who was missing what a husband has to offer. There was a huge gap in their lives because there was no man in the home.

I've researched families and especially the role of the father in the family for my master's thesis. I grew up in a typical but dysfunctional situation. Dad was home, and he was a good guy—a great athlete, a strong masculine figure—but he wasn't emotionally or relationally "present." In addition to his issues with alcoholism, he took a passive approach to being a husband and father. He became so dependent, my mom had to pick out what clothes he would wear to work. My mother ran the home.

I remember coming home after school one day, and I could tell Dad was really ticked off.

"What's wrong?" I asked.

"I'm hungry!"

"Isn't there food in the refrigerator?"

"Well, yeah, but your mom isn't here to fix it for me."

All I can remember thinking is how pathetic that was—that a grown man was paralyzed by the fact that no one was there to pull some food out of the fridge and fix it for him. But over the years since then, I've realized that, in less dramatic ways, that isn't unusual. Men are missing in action in a shocking number of homes.

I don't mean that as a slam against anyone in particular. It is a large cultural trend that has been building over the last several decades. I understand that life is hard and that it isn't easy to stand firm against shifting social dynamics. But there is a profile of manhood in Scripture that men are called to live out, and it builds up women, children, and the family unit as a whole. When men fit into that biblical portrait, they become the strength of society.

> *When men fit into that biblical portrait, they become the strength of society.*

I see absent-father families as one of the two major consequences in this evolution of the American male. The other is the impact of these changing roles. Whether for reasons no family can avoid (like war or illness) or because of bad decisions and dysfunctional relationships, the absenteeism of American fathers has left a huge hole in the lives of many children.

The negative impact on families caused such concern that the US government conducted a study on child development called Code Blue. In its evaluation of adolescents, it stated: "Never before has one generation of American teenagers been less healthy, less cared for, or less prepared for life."[4] This observation was followed with the note that this situation occurred "in one of the most affluent and privileged nations in the history of the world."[5]

Another study concluded that boys suffer more than girls from the absence or noninvolvement of a father. They are twice as likely to drop out of school, twice as likely to go to jail, and four times as likely to need treatment for emotional and behavioral problems as boys with engaged, at-home fathers.[6] Harvard psychologist William Pollack, author of *Real Boys*, says divorce is difficult for all children but particularly for males. "The basic problem is the lack of discipline and supervision in a father's absence and his unavailability to teach what it means to be a man."[7] So homes with absent or disengaged fathers beget homes with future absent or disengaged fathers.

Sociologist Peter Karl notes that 80 percent of a boy's time in his childhood years is spent with women. "They don't know how to act as men when they grow up. When that happens, the relationship between the sexes is directly affected and men become helpless and more like big kids."[8]

My mental picture of that dynamic is the man who dons a backward baseball cap and the jersey of some twenty-five-year-old star athlete to play fantasy football. His manhood comes from playing and pretending. And why not? He may have never been around a man who leads, provides, and lives with courage. Somewhere between *Friends* and *Homer Simpson*, he never got a picture of what it means to be a man. The roles have blurred.

Not Missing, but Present

If you are a woman, you may wonder if it is even possible for your husband or son to learn how to be a "real man."

He genuinely may have never been given a picture of biblical manhood. That's a legitimate concern, and much of this book will aim to address it.

A psychologist and author in San Francisco, Pierre Mornell recognized the same concern in many of his clients nearly four decades ago. He was amazed at how many wives of powerful men in the financial districts of San Francisco were coming to see him for counseling. The book recounts multiple stories of wives whose husbands drove into the city daily to lead major financial institutions where they exercise power, strategy, and focus to achieve multimillion- and even billion-dollar deals. Yet they returned home only to be couch potatoes or bury their faces in the *Wall Street Journal*.

Mornell writes, "A man who is passive at home is often extremely active at work. On the job he is energetic and assertive. Indeed he may be absolutely dynamic. And yet as the old saying about the salesman goes, 'He may be a tiger in the territory, but he's a mouse in the house.'"[9]

> Just because a man is in the home does not mean he is in the home in a meaningful way.

He described this phenomenon in a bestseller called *Passive Men, Wild Women*. His thesis was that this behavior in men creates "wild," frustrated, angry women. I would suggest that it also creates very confused children. Men in that situation may not be as absent as the MIA father of the girl I dated in high school, but they produce similar results. Just because a man is in the home does not mean he is in the home in a meaningful way. Boys and girls need fathers who are not missing in action.

Avoiding the Two PCs

At this point, if you're a man and feeling discouraged, or a woman and feeling discouraged *with* men, I want to remind you that trust is powerful. God has always redeemed people groups through the hands of a few committed men and women who choose to believe, obey, and swim upstream. Later we'll discuss practical ways to turn the tide, but let's be careful to avoid the common pitfalls.

Society has tried to compensate for MIA men, and it has come up with two extremes we want to avoid. I call them the two PCs.

One is the modern politically correct image of manhood, which says anything goes—any lifestyle, any family unit, any alternative. In light of what we have seen from Scripture and research, I think we can agree that this PC definition of manhood is not an effective one. It doesn't work.

The other PC is pseudo-Christian. It's a knee-jerk reaction to politically correct manhood, and it shows up as the image of a narrow-minded, bigoted, I'm-in-control, I'm-the-head-of-the-house, Bible-thumping stereotype. The old chauvinistic caricature of the "man of the house" who has to insist on his authority and make everyone else submit to him is not a biblical image. If you have to thump your chest and tell people you're in charge, you aren't. If you have to demand respect, you don't have it. That picture of manhood is absolutely not what the Bible teaches.

I grew up without knowing what it meant to be a man. I just did what my father had done. I figured out how to be a good athlete and pretend to be a man. Then I became a Christian.

I had to completely relearn manhood, and in some ways I started from scratch. It's a lifelong process, and it goes against the grain of our culture. But the blueprint has been there for a long time: it was perfectly embodied in Jesus, and it is explained in Ephesians 5.

We can even become the examples and role models for the next generation that we wish we would have had in ours.

In chapter 2, we saw what real manhood looks like; in this one, we've seen the enormous obstacles standing in the way of our ideals. But those obstacles are not insurmountable. In fact, with an admission that we can't do this in our own power and a resolve to trust God's promises and encourage one another, we can overcome them. We can even become the examples and role models for the next generation that we wish we would have had in ours. We just need a few tools and a lot of encouragement.

Bringing It Home: Now What?

By and large, we are the product of the significant people in our lives. Modeling is the most powerful influence in human development and behavior. We all grow up in certain homes, and without exception, we speak, eat, form traditions, get perspectives, and develop identities very much as our parents did. The way we look at the world is shaped by the key influencers in our lives. Unfortunately, it's rare to meet men who say something like, "I want to be a godly man like my dad."

So for those of us who didn't grow up as believers and didn't have a strong, godly father, what are we to do? Let me give you a few key suggestions that have helped me become the kind of man described in Ephesians 5.

Find a godly mentor. More is caught than taught.

In my early years, coaches filled the role of a father figure when my dad was absent. They taught me the disciplines of manhood and believed in me. After trusting Christ, I met Dave, the bricklayer I wrote about in the introduction. He discipled me during college and modeled what it looked like to date his wife, love his kids, and practice biblical priorities. Since that time, I've prayed for, looked for, and found men in every season to help me become the kind of man who loves his family well.

Start or join a men's small group. It's impossible to make it on your own.

Our wives can be wonderful friends and companions, but they don't fully understand how we think, where we struggle, or the fears that hold us back. From those early days until now, some four decades later, I've committed to doing life with a group of men. These have been honest, raw, gutsy, biblical, heart-to-heart relationships of love and support, and they have been safe places to share my biggest failures and strong places to give me the kick in the rear I needed whenever I started to drift.

Renew your mind. You are the product of your thought life.

Don't just read the Bible and great books on manhood and marriage. You should be doing that anyway. Every day we are bombarded by messages—on sports talk radio, on the financial page, in movies, in video games, and in certain negative relationships—that constantly work against our desire to become the men we long to be. To be a man of God, you have to stop the negative flow that creates desires and temptations that pull you away from God and from your efforts to love your wife sacrificially, intentionally, and sensitively. You have to replace that input with positive and inspiring thoughts about the rewards of a great marriage. You can fill your mind with those kinds of thoughts through books, movies, and relationships that inspire you and encourage you to be an Ephesians 5 man and husband.

Tools for Becoming an Ephesians 5 Man

With that in mind, here are some practical tools to help you.

The Daily Walk Bible is the easiest and clearest Bible I've found that provides context and understanding for those who don't know much about the Bible or who want to grasp the overall message and meaning. For the first fifteen years of my Christian life, I read it every year, and I have dipped back into it multiple times since.

True Spirituality: Becoming a Romans 12 Christian is a book I wrote about my journey in understanding what it means to be a disciple of Christ and how to practically follow him in the five key relationships of your life. The greatest gift I have ever given my wife is becoming more like Christ, but for years I didn't really know how that worked or how to go about it. I think some of these lessons from my own journey may be a great help to you. This content is available in multiple formats: free MP3s, CDs, or videos at

truespiritualityonline.org.

The Five Love Languages: The Secret to Love that Lasts by Gary Chapman is a perennial bestseller I believe every man should read tomorrow if he hasn't already. It's a very simple and quick read, but it will open your eyes to the way your wife and other people think. For years, I nearly drove myself crazy trying to love my wife in ways that didn't connect with her. After I read this book and learned her "language of love," tons of frustration turned into positive emotions. I learned how to make deposits instead of constant withdrawals in the love bank of our relationship. It greatly improved how we relate to each other.

Those resources can help every man become a better husband, but, of course, this book isn't only about how men can make their marriages better. We have focused on the roles and characteristics of men in the preceding two chapters because men have the ability to set the tone for everything else in marriage and family relationships. But men and women are in this relationship together. The roles and characteristics of women are just as critical to the beauty of the dance. In the next two chapters, we will explore the wonders and opportunities of biblical femininity.

_____ **Questions for Reflection and Discussion** _____

1. In what ways have you seen the definition of manhood change during the course of your lifetime?

2. Think of one man you have looked up to as a model of manhood. What characteristics does he have? Where does he fit in the cultural evolution of masculine ideals? How well do you think he embodies the biblical idea of manhood? Why?

3. In what ways, if any, have you experienced or witnessed absentee fatherhood? What about passive fatherhood? What effects of this phenomenon have you observed?

4. If you are a man, what is your response to the examples and research presented in this chapter? Do they discourage you? Confirm your beliefs? Motivate you to make any changes? Why?

5. What next step do you sense God would have you take to become the man and husband he has designed you to become?

6. Who could help you on this journey? What man or men would be willing to be a "band of brothers" with you as you move toward biblical manhood?

4

Is There a Woman in the House?

Submit to one another out of reverence for Christ.

Wives, submit yourselves to your own husbands as you do to the Lord. For the husband is the head of the wife as Christ is the head of the church, his body, of which he is the Savior. Now as the church submits to Christ, so also wives should submit to their husbands in everything.

Husbands, love your wives, just as Christ loved the church and gave himself up for her to make her holy, cleansing her by the washing with water through the word, and to present her to himself as a radiant church, without stain or wrinkle or any other blemish, but holy and blameless. In this same way, husbands ought to love their wives as their own bodies. He who loves his wife loves himself. After all, no one ever hated their own body, but they feed and care for their body, just as Christ does the church—for we are members of his body.

"For this reason a man will leave his father and mother and be united to his wife, and the two will become one flesh."

> This is a profound mystery—but I am talking about Christ
> and the church. However, each one of you also must love
> his wife as he loves himself, and the wife must respect her
> husband.
>
> —Ephesians 5:21–33

t's an age-old stereotype, isn't it? Men are in charge, and women are supposed to submit to them. Some have claimed that to be Christian teaching. But as we have seen, it is really a distortion of what the Bible says. It's an abuse of Christian truth that ignores context and focuses on only a few isolated, misinterpreted phrases. Men and societies with an inflated sense of patriarchy have for centuries exploited Scripture to control women.

The fact that counterfeit teaching has been around for a long time, though, should not keep us away from the real thing. The truth is that mutual submission is the background of our entire discussion of male and female roles. Both men and women look to God to say, "I'm going to submit to you and do life your way, according to your Word." Then they turn to each other and say, "I'm going to seek your needs and your well-being above my own." In God's economy for human relationships, this mutual submission is where everything begins.

Marriage is never about establishing your own rights or telling your mate what he or she is supposed to do. God's words to men are directed toward men, not toward women to use as a weapon against their men; and God's words to women are directed toward women, not toward men to use as a weapon against their women. When each person takes the words directed specifically at them to heart, beautiful things happen. When we cross lines and direct those words at each other, we stir up conflict.

The questions to ask your spouse are, "How can I make you more successful? How can I love you more deeply? How can I serve you well?" Those questions fit under the umbrella of mutual submission. We are given a vivid picture of it in Philippians 2:3–4:

> Do nothing from selfishness or empty conceit, but with hu-mility of mind regard one another as more important than yourselves; do not merely look out for your own personal interests, but also for the interests of others. (NASB)

This teaching is not addressed specifically to men or women. It is written to all the members of the church at Philippi. In Christian thought, submission is not an exception or for one group of people; it is the norm. This is how everyone should treat each other. In fact, the following verses (Phil. 2:5–8) command us to have this other-centered attitude toward everyone just as Christ did. We, like Jesus, are to take up the role of servant, and applying this to the marriage relation-ship should not be surprising at all.

As unto Christ

We saw a couple chapters ago that this Christlike attitude is where the dance of marriage begins, and it started with the man stepping up. But the dance requires some more clarity of roles. What is the woman's role? How does she make the dance beautiful?

Let's look at the choreography again, this time specifically with an eye on what it says to women:

> Wives, submit yourselves to your own husbands as you do to the Lord. For the husband is the head of the wife as Christ is the head of the church, his body, of which he is the Savior. Now as the church submits to Christ, so also wives should submit to their husbands in everything. (Eph. 5:22–24)

The word "submit" is not a negative word. We will see that it has nothing to do with inferiority or inequality and everything to do with function, structure, and roles. As the church is subject to Christ, wives ought to be subject "to their husbands in everything" (v. 24). If a man loves his wife as Christ loves the church, it is not difficult to submit to him, in the true sense of submission.

Submission does not mean saying, "Yes, dear," to whatever your husband says. Scripture does not tell wives that they need to be *passive*. That is an extreme reaction to trying to be in control, and it goes too far in the opposite direction. A wife is to step into the marriage relationship—not step over her husband—with strength and respect. She is an equal partner. A partner who submits to the righteous leadership of the other partner—her husband.

Equal Standing, Different Roles

What exactly does this mean? First, couples must understand that marriage is not a fifty-fifty proposition.

Every organization—whether it's a business, the military, a school, a club, or even a small group—has some sort of structure and leadership. Ultimately, someone is responsible. That does not mean members are not equal as human beings or that some members are more valuable than others. It does mean, however, that some people carry more weight of responsibility than others.

This applies to marriage too. God says that just as Christ is the head of the church, the man is head of the family—spiritually, emotionally, relationally.

Again, this has nothing to do with value or equality. We know this because the same principle is discussed in 1 Corinthians 11:3, where Paul writes that "Christ is the head of every man, and the man is the head of a woman, and God is the head of Christ" (NASB). Jesus submitted himself to the Father, but the Father, the Son, and the Spirit are equal in essence and in value. There is no higher or lower in the Trinity, but there are different roles and functions.

Christ, being equal to the Father, chose to submit to him because of their different roles. Likewise, a wife first must submit to her husband, not because of any difference in value or importance, but because of the distinction of their marriage roles.

Second, a wife must voluntarily support her husband from the heart as an act of obedience to God. The key word is "voluntarily." This is not a burden to bear; it is a choice that comes from a joyful heart. When a woman believes that God has put this man in her life ultimately for her good, she doesn't have to worry that he might mess everything up for her. Ultimately, it's God, not her husband, who's in control and sovereign over her life.

Third, a wife must believe that submission—responding as a skillful dance partner to her husband's initiatives rather than competing against him—is her greatest ally in bringing about positive change. It is her way of cooperating with God's design in choreographing the steps of her marriage and her family.

R.E.S.P.E.C.T.

After Paul's words on marriage and the responsibilities of the husband, he concludes the passage in Ephesians 5 with the wife's response to her husband's selfless love: "The wife must see to it that she respects her husband" (v. 33 NASB). The Greek word for "respect" in this verse comes from the root word "phobos," from which we get our word "phobia," but it doesn't have the same connotation. It means reverence, not fear.

Many women do not realize how deeply men need to feel honored and respected. A man feels loved when he is encouraged—when his wife steps into his life and communicates by words and actions, "I believe in you." When she willingly supports and encourages his leadership, she is making a profound statement that will resonate deeply in his heart. She is acknowledging the position God has put him in and respecting his God-given role. Even though he may feel that he has been given an impossible standard to live up to, she is on his side to help him be successful.

When a man loses the respect of his wife, he will shut down, be passive-aggressive, bury himself in his fantasy teams or his work, and have no idea what's going on in the hearts of his wife and children. It is devastating for a man not to be honored and respected.

If this has been a problem in the past—if he had a father who did not affirm him or a history of relationships in which he has been torn down—he may no longer believe in himself. He will seek affirmation wherever he can get it—by driving a hot car, getting a scholarship, dating a beautiful girl, getting degrees, making a team, nabbing a high-salary job, acing a project, and on and on.

> *Every man has a desperate need for his wife to step in and believe in him.*

Affirmation feels like love, but it isn't, and it doesn't fill a man up. A husband will be on a never-ending search for it unless he gets it from his wife. Every man has a desperate need for his wife to step in and believe in him.

His Insecurity, Her Strength

The fear of failure is one of the greatest fears every man secretly lives with. That's one reason men are such experts at overcompensating. We focus on the things we know we can be good at, like our work or sports or hobbies. We know what we are doing there.

But if you ask the average man how his family is doing spiritually, you may get an awkward response. The same is true if you ask him how sensitive and caring he is in guiding his children through their challenges. We men can be awfully insecure on these points, even though they are part of our God-given design.

Women often respond to that insecurity by taking the reins of the family and trying to control their husbands and children. This ultimately sabotages the marriage. So God tells wives to submit—not because the husband is inherently better or more important, and not because he is more capable or qualified, but because her submission to him builds him up and empowers him to lead.

Where men are to *step up* in the dance of marriage, women are to *step in* with support, affirmation, and encouragement, building up their husbands with strength and respect so they can lead their families in righteousness.

Antiquated Thought?

You can imagine how well this goes over in some circles, especially in light of today's social and political climate. Imagine meeting a woman at a coffee shop and having a conversation with her about this:

"What are you reading?" she asks.

"A book about marriage."

"What are you learning?"

"Well, the past few chapters have been pretty cool. They say my man is supposed to step up, lead, provide, and even lay down his life for me."

"Wow, that's great. Maybe I should read it too."

"Well, you should see what it says about women first," you warn.

"Really? What does it say?"

"It uses the *S* word."

"Huh?"

"'Submission.' My husband is responsible to be a servant leader, and then I bring all my strengths and gifts into the relationship. We talk and share our opinions. But if we get to an impasse, I'm supposed to defer to him and submit."

"Wow, that is so antiquated. I can't believe there are still people who think that way."

And it's true that this is extremely politically incorrect—if we look at it through the lens of the twenty-first century.

But imagine being a man who has grown up in an ancient culture about the time Paul was writing. If you're a new Christian, you may be nicer to your wife than most men of this era are to theirs, and perhaps you have a pretty good marriage. But you've grown up thinking women are just a step up from slaves or are primarily objects of pleasure. Many of the people you know have been divorced numerous times, and it's not considered a big deal. So imagine how shocked you would be when you go to a church in Ephesus and hear a letter from a well-known apostle being read to the congregation, and it starts talking about mutual submission—not to a friend or colleague but to your wife. A woman.

This apostle actually considers her to be a coheir of God's grace and an equal in God's eyes. You are supposed to love her sacrificially and maybe even lay down your life for her. Paul comes across as incredibly progressive, very liberal, and downright radical. It's hard to believe someone would elevate women to a status equal to yours as a man.

Do you see the difference perspective can make? At the time, Paul could be considered a liberator, just as Jesus had been a few years earlier. The Bible elevates both partners. When it talks about submission, it is always in the context of a sovereign God who created roles that fit together. When each person does his or her part, they form a rich and healthy relationship.

Taking Control Alone

Our culture today has distorted that perspective. A woman wants to feel secure and protected. When she doesn't, fear takes over and she seeks control. As we will see in the next chapter, radical feminism exploited injustices—many very real ones—and embraced the desire to control to the point that many feminists not only believe they no longer need men but also hate men and blame them for most of society's problems.

That theme still runs pretty strongly through some areas of our culture, and I've seen some very bright, well-educated women buy into it unconsciously and start down a path that ends with them hating their own lives. That distorted perception of men does not lead to a healthy place or a rich and fulfilling relationship.

I sat next to an extremely intelligent young woman on a plane recently. She was in her late twenties, spoke five languages, and was flying into Atlanta to interview with an airline for a very high-powered position that would require her to travel all over the world. We had a great conversation. She said she had been married for about a year and a half, so I asked her what her husband thought about the possibility of her traveling so much. She said he was excited about it. I asked how things were going to work in their marriage if she was gone two or three weeks at a time. "Oh, it will be fine. We only see each other for half a day each week now," she explained.

"What do you mean?"

She told me about his job, which paid him a lot of money but kept him on a tight schedule. Then she told me about her job, which also paid a lot of money but kept her busy. "So he has later hours, and I work an early shift, so we only see each other for about a half day on Saturday anyway, and we're both pretty tired."

That's the kind of living arrangement their choices had led to, and it's hard to believe anyone would make that kind of arrangement on purpose. But they had both unconsciously bought into the cultural ideal of making a lot of money, moving up the ladder, and squeezing in a marriage on the side. I suspect she will wake up in about fifteen years and question it all. If this couple has a child, she will experience all the natural pangs and urges of nurturing and motherhood, but those urges will have to compete with years of investing in a high-stakes career, a two-income lifestyle, and the status and self-image that go along with that life. It's going to be difficult to manage that crisis. And tragically, the promises of happiness that wealth, power, and travel make will never satisfy the deepest yearnings of her heart.

Intentional Choices

You have to be clear on the identity God has given you and what really matters. That will mean making some hard decisions. Some women are able to pursue a career for a while and then embrace marriage and motherhood with ease. Some choose never to go the marriage-and-family route. But for those who are trying to do it all, it can be very stressful and often unfulfilling.

A couple needs to be very intentional about who is going to work in which seasons of life and know how to live out their God-given roles. They need to ask the hard questions of how their relationship will play out practically in terms of jobs and raising a family. The best scenario for fifteen years down the road is not having parallel fast-track careers that allow you to see each other once or twice a week; instead, the best scenario is having a rich and rewarding relationship that is stable and secure and satisfies your needs at the deepest levels.

And if that scenario includes children, providing a stable and secure environment where they can also experience love

and deeply secure relationships becomes part of the equation. You want your children to grow up and still desire a
relationship with you, to be able to look back and appreciate
the sacrifice and investments you have made for them. But
couples who try to balance it all without making any major
sacrifices are going to end up making the biggest sacrifice
of all. They are going to miss out on the fullness of what
marriage and family can be. It's no accident that attempt-
ing to "do it all" and "have it all" among Christians and
non-Christians alike has resulted in fractured families and
painful, life-altering divorces.

As a pastor, I've never done a funeral that focused on how
many languages the deceased spoke, how many promotions
he or she got, or how much money that person made. The
letters behind the names, the stock portfolios, the professional accolades—none of that comes up when everyone is
sitting around talking about this person who is no longer
with us. People talk about two things: relationships and love.

I've also never heard of people on their deathbed talking
about their professional regrets. It's always about how they
wish they'd spent more time with their family, parented their
children differently, or appreciated their spouse when they
had the chance. At the end of life, relational issues come to
the forefront and all the other pursuits fade into the background. People finally realize what's important. Sadly, sometimes they realize too late.

God has a plan for that—for men and women to relate to
each other in the healthiest and most satisfying ways and
to share the love between them with the next generation by

raising children in that same nurturing, fulfilling environment. Part of that equation is for women to step into the marriage relationship to support, affirm, and encourage their husbands with strength and respect so that their husbands can lead their families in righteousness.

The Power of Submission

For that to happen, women need to take a huge step of faith and believe that submission is actually their greatest ally in seeing the change they want to see in the men they love. Most women I know would like for their husbands to be more romantic, or more responsible, or more intentional in the way they lead, provide, and communicate. They already know that nagging doesn't work. Neither do arguing or passive-aggressive moods.

What if God said, "If that's what you really want to see in the life of your husband, try submitting to him and see how he changes"? Would you be able to trust him on that—not for a day or two, but over enough time to see genuine change?

The issue is not whether your husband deserves your voluntary, joyful submission; there are plenty of days when he does not, and he probably knows that. Nor is the issue that he will make better decisions than you; he may not. This is a trust issue with God, who blesses marriage and has, in one way or another, put you and your husband together in a committed relationship.

When a man feels honored, respected, affirmed, and encouraged, something happens inside him. It may take time, but

God begins to work in his heart. The change you are looking for begins to take shape.

Theresa's Three Truths

I can interpret Scripture and teach these principles, but obviously I've never been on the other side of this teaching—listening to it as a woman. I know the truth, but I don't really know the practical implications.

So I asked my wife how a woman perceives this teaching. She pulls this off beautifully, without being a pushover or being manipulative. What goes on inside a woman's mind when she tries to apply this "outdated" concept in real life? How does it work in her heart? Here's what Theresa said:

> This hasn't always been easy for me, but I've found three things that have really helped me live out submission in the biblical sense.
>
> First, I feel secure because I trust Chip to have my best interests in mind. I certainly don't believe he's perfect; I know his flaws better than anyone, and I will not hesitate to disagree with him. But I also know his heart and that he's on my side. I know that he will give careful thought and prayer to every decision.
>
> Second, I love the Lord and his Word, and it is my heart's desire to obey God. I ask God to shape my heart, I lean on his strength, and I claim the promises from his Word when I don't understand and don't feel like submitting. I am convinced that God will take up my cause because he cares for me.

The third thing is clear communication. It gives me great confidence to know that Chip and I will talk through everything. In our marriage, we have worked hard on this. We talk nearly every day, share our thoughts, struggles, dreams, and how we are processing decisions we need to make and issues we need to deal with. I'm confident, even though we may go through significant conflict, that I'll really be heard and that I can trust Chip's heart.

> I am convinced that God will take up my cause because he cares for me.

I believe that these three concepts, if embraced by both husband and wife, will help women accept their role in a biblical marriage. It's been a real journey and a process for me to understand what it takes to build a safe environment in which Theresa and I can work through difficult issues and come to resolutions that we can both live with.

Stating Her Case Strongly

Theresa and I have had some pretty big areas of tension over the years, as nearly all couples do. One of ours was how to discipline our children. Another has been taking care of the home—maintaining and repairing the physical environment. We've had major challenges with in-laws, communication, frequency of and perspective on sex, and where and how we spend our time. We see these things very differently, and Theresa is very honest about how difficult it has been to submit sometimes, especially when she considers something to be a major issue and I consider it a minor one.

Some of these issues have evaporated as we've matured, but every couple has ongoing issues. The most difficult for us have been those rare times when we've had major decisions to make and didn't see eye to eye. We have moved a lot, and we haven't always agreed on where God was leading us (or if he was leading us somewhere different at all). Like many wives, Theresa likes to feel settled. Both men and women may experience this, but I believe women are more often reluctant to leave friends, schools, and other social connections behind.

She has cried out to God more than once to claim his promise in Romans 8:32: "He who did not spare his own Son, but gave him up for us all—how will he not also, along with him, graciously give us all things?" She knows that wherever we are and however uncertain life seems to be, God is going to freely give her what she needs.

I cannot express how much I value Theresa's willingness to be supportive and encouraging as she follows my lead, but I equally value her willingness to express how she feels, raise the difficult questions, and state her case with passion and strength.

That does not feel threatening to me because I know if she buries her true feelings, they are going to come out sideways in other areas. Resentment will grow and eventually come to the surface. It isn't easy for her to follow along when she is concerned I may be doing the wrong thing, or to have a good attitude in the process, but she gets there. She trusts my heart, and she trusts God to be sovereign over every human decision.

What Happens If He Does Not Lead?

When women don't trust their husband's heart, or fear that he is not leading well, they face a formidable challenge. Ideally, a wife follows a husband who is loving her sacrificially as Christ loves the church and is always praying and seeking godly wisdom as he leads. But what if he doesn't? How do you follow from a place of insecurity? How do you let go of the reins when you fear that things will fall apart as soon as you do?

That's a really difficult situation, but it isn't beyond God's provision.

Women have a very natural desire to run their homes and families well, but that desire often turns into a sense of control. This issue of submission is one area in which God will allow that sense of control to be tested and challenged.

Are you willing to let go and trust God? That's the real issue, and it isn't an easy one, but it is important. Remember that in any situation, God cares for you. He is ultimately your defender. He will take up your cause in whatever situation you find yourself in if you submit it to him.

Prayer is your best strategy in any area of life, especially this one. Pray for your husband, knowing that God can change his heart. Pray with the expectation that God will change circumstances if necessary.

And then, in faith, give God room to work in your husband, in your circumstances, and in your own heart. Sometimes people pray for change and then allow no space for it to happen. They keep acting as the agent of change even when their intervention is not helping. Give God space, time, and your trust, then wait to see what he does.

You might be surprised how hands-on he can be when you determine to be hands-off and trust him. We'll talk about how to do this in a later chapter, but for now,

> *Are you willing to let go and trust God?*

purpose in your heart to refuse to live in fear of what "might happen" if you entrust your husband and his role to Christ. At times it can be really hard to discern, especially if your husband isn't currently walking with Lord, what is wise to submit to and what is not. The appendix in this book is written by a friend who specializes in helping women who find themselves in difficult situations.

Wanting the Best for the Marriage

Theresa's motto for her approach to our marriage is from Proverbs 31:12: "She brings him good, not harm, all the days of her life." Behind every discussion and every decision, she is asking, "Am I doing him good, or am I doing him harm?"

Sometimes doing good for me means submitting to something she doesn't necessarily agree with. Sometimes it means refusing to take responsibility for something that is really on my shoulders.

But in every case, she wants the best not only for our marriage and for herself but also for me. And, of course, I want that for her. When all those steps come together, the dance can be a beautiful experience. But remember, as we learn to dance, we often step on each other's feet. In the next chapter, we'll take a look at how this works out in real life.

—————— Questions for Reflection and Discussion ——————

1. How have abuses and distortions of the concept of submission made it difficult for a woman to function according to God's design?

2. In what ways does the context of mutual submission make a wife's submission to her husband more reasonable than many people assume?

3. In what ways does a wife's role meet her husband's needs? What can a husband do to create a safe environment for his wife to fulfill her role?

4. If you are a woman, what is the most challenging aspect of your role as described by Ephesians 5? What mental shifts would you need to make to trust God's process and your part in his choreography?

5. If you are a man, what changes do you need to make to help your wife step more fully into her role in the relationship?

5

The Evolution
of the American Woman

Before we go any further, I want you to know I'm deeply aware that the preceding chapter may have been difficult to swallow. If you're thirty-five or younger, it may have sounded like a foreign language from another planet. No matter how diplomatically and sensitively I present it, and no matter how much biblical support I use to communicate a woman's role in marriage, it still comes across as counter to our culture's pervasive beliefs. It is difficult for many women to fathom.

So I asked my wife to share her perspective and experience in living out a role that is so at odds with today's cultural values.

Over the past several years, I have had the privilege of leading a Bible study in my home called *Five Aspects of Woman: A*

Biblical Theology of Femininity, written by Barbara Mouser. It has been around for many years but is not very well known. We do an in-depth study of what the Bible says about the feminine gender. Every time I go through it, I become more aware of how wonderful it is to be a woman in the way God created us to be. God did not create us to be servants or to be used and abused. He created us in his very own image with a much bigger picture in mind of who we are. We are the crown of his creation, and we are made to reflect the relationship that Christ has with his treasured church. God has given us the authority and responsibility to nurture, rule over, and bear fruit in what he has entrusted to us.

God's truth about femininity is the same for every woman. In my group right now, there are young singles, older singles, young married women, engaged women, career women, stay-at-home moms, and grandmothers. We come from all over the world, and we have varying levels of education. Some of us come from very difficult backgrounds, and some come from great Christian homes. We are all made in God's image, he loves us dearly, and we all have a purpose to fulfill in this life that will bring glory to him.

In our first Bible study session, one of the questions is, "Do you like being a woman?" I am always concerned when many group members respond that they do not necessarily like being a woman. They believe that men, throughout history and still today, have had more opportunities, more pay, and more recognition, and they have taken advantage of and oppressed women. Many women are fed up and get mad and fight back, as the radical feminist movement encourages us to do. Those of us who are not radical also feel the tension and challenges of being a woman in the twenty-first century.

Yet as women study God's truth about what it means to be a woman and they begin to get the "big picture" and the "right picture" of who they are—as they see themselves through God's eyes and understand his great plan for them—many learn to fully appreciate being a woman. We are not doormats for men to wipe their feet on! We are made in the image of God with gifts and abilities, women who have been given responsibility, capability, and authority to change our world and bring great glory to him.

I am amazed by the stories Theresa shares with me about the transformation in these women's lives. They are wrestling with the big questions that women face in the twenty-first century: "What am I supposed to do with my life? I have so many voices and so many expectations about what it means to be a woman. How does a woman know what is most important, what to give her life to, and why?"

As their identity gets rooted in who God made them to be, they begin to have a new confidence. As they embrace what makes a woman flourish and discover what she needs to get and what she needs to give, they peel away old paradigms and prisons of external expectations. People from liberal and conservative backgrounds surrender their preconceived notions and get a fresh, new vision of what it means to be a woman. The positive changes that follow in them and in their relationships are amazing to behold.

So before we talk about practical ways to be an Ephesians 5 wife, I think it will be helpful to discuss the evolution of the American woman. As with the changes men have experienced, the cultural transformation that has occurred in the last fifty to sixty years with regard to women has made biblical marriage more difficult than ever before.

The Evolution of the American Woman

While I was researching material for this book, I had a conversation on an airplane with a young woman—a different one from the woman I talked with in chapter 4. She had been thinking a lot about what to do with her life. She had just finished grad school, was already pretty far along a successful career path, and was about to get engaged. "But," she said, "there are so many voices in my head, I just don't know what to do."

"What do you mean?" I asked.

"Well, I've finished school, spent all this money on a degree, and have a great career, but I want to be married and have kids. I'm already thirty-two, and if we get married and wait three or four years, I'll be in my midthirties when I have children, so we probably won't have many. And I really want to be home with my kids to raise them, but my friends tell me that I'd be wasting my education. I'm not sure my fiancé and I are on the same page. My mom says one thing, my aunt says another, and then I read about people and the choices they have made—it's like all of a sudden, I'm wondering what it means to be a woman. What am I supposed to do with my life?"

I think a lot of women have similar thoughts, though many may not articulate these feelings as clearly as this young woman did. She was right about the voices speaking to her;

they come from all directions, and some of them are pretty critical of motherhood.

I've encountered an attitude, I think especially common in Europe—motivated by concerns about boosting national economies—that undermines mothers staying at home. In fact, I remember hearing the term "waster" applied to mothers who don't work outside the home. It seems that struggling economies in some countries are more important than strengthening families.

Wasters? That attitude is blind to the noneconomic factors of a woman staying at home with her kids.

A stay-at-home mom is there for the first six to eight years of a child's life, when 80 percent of a child's brain and personality is being formed—how they feel about themselves, their confidence, their moral values, their sense of identity, their understanding of their place in the world.[1] Some people would encourage women to completely outsource their childcare during those critical years—to pay someone else minimum wage to handle the most critical years of a human being's life. I'm not saying it is wrong for women to work outside the home or to expect men to share in the parenting load (unlike in generations past). My point is that we need to recognize the almost universal devaluation of motherhood and its impact on the family and society. And all I want to say is, "How is that working?"

To understand how we got to this point, we need to look back at the bigger historical picture and especially the last few decades. Womanhood has its blessings, the miracle of childbirth and motherhood among them. But womanhood also comes with its own set of challenges, many of them deeply embedded in cultural biases and perceptions. In this case, we're going even further back in time to examine some of the roots of the negative perception of women. And I'll begin not with the Bible but with the contexts it came from—ancient Jewish, Greek, and Roman cultures.

The Old Testament is not disparaging toward women, but Jewish culture during the time of Jesus had a pretty low view of them. Women were often viewed as servants or property. At every stage in life, a woman was considered to be under the care and supervision of a man—a father, a husband, or a son—and those who weren't (e.g., widows, especially childless ones) were considered especially vulnerable. Women were not considered in Jewish law to be valid witnesses—one of the main subthemes behind the disciples' doubt over the testimony of the women who had come back from Jesus's empty tomb. One attitude of men during that time, expressed in Jewish prayer books in later centuries (and even today), is reflected in a daily prayer in which a man thanks God for not making him a Gentile, a slave, or a woman. As much as men may have valued their wives, they considered them lower in status.

The Greeks were often worse. Marriage was arranged, divorce was easy (for the husband), and women were generally forced into one of three roles.

> We have courtesans for pleasure, we have concubines for the sake of daily cohabitation, and we have wives for the purpose of having children legitimately and being faithful guardians of our household affairs.[2]

As this quote from a fifth-century BC Athenian orator suggests, men found their pleasures outside of marriage: fornication and prostitution were rampant. Greek men had a wife for housekeeping and bearing legitimate children, another woman for meeting sexual and companion needs, and access to prostitutes when they wanted to satisfy urges at other times.

When Paul writes in 1 Timothy 3:2 that an overseer must be the husband of one wife, he is not talking about men in a second or third marriage after their wives have died. The phrase he uses literally means "a one-woman man" because many Greeks were three- or four-women men, having relationships with several women even when they were married to only one.[3]

Among Romans, divorce was much more common. Jerome, translator of the Bible into Latin in the AD 400s, wrote of one Roman woman who was married for the twenty-third time, and she was her husband's twenty-first wife.[4] That was by no means standard, but neither was it uncommon. To some, marriage was nothing more than legalized prostitution.

Of course, injustice toward women is not confined to ancient times or traditional cultures. Historically, the world has not been a great place for women. Rights and freedoms have not been fair or equitable between the sexes at most times and in most places. That's a historical fact. Women could not vote in the United States until 1920; in Switzerland, they could not vote until 1971. In 1960s America, a woman who wanted to rent an apartment or get credit had to have a male relative sign for her. Apparently, women were not considered responsible enough to pay their bills.

As you know, we have experienced a huge cultural transformation. Women have gone well beyond voting and purchasing on credit; many run businesses, serve in legislatures, invent new technologies, run for president, and excel at law and medicine. In fact, there are more women than men in medical school in the United States right now.[5] Women's movements have accomplished a lot in a relatively short time.

Feminism versus Radical Feminism

"Feminism" is not a negative word. It may be a controversial one, depending on your perspective, but it is not bad. *Merriam-Webster's Collegiate Dictionary* defines it as "the theory of the political, economic, and social equality of the sexes." People may argue over the application of that definition, but the core principle should be well accepted. Equality between men and women is a good thing.

But feminism and *radical* feminism are two different things. Somehow the movement for women's rights transitioned in the '70s from gaining equality to labeling men as the source of all injustices. A magazine playing on the acronym for the National Organization for Women once declared that "NOW is the time to take back control of our lives. . . . NOW is the time to drop the boot heel in the groin of patriarchy, NOW is the time to fight back. No god, no master, no laws."[6] Women's studies programs were birthed in the '70s at women's colleges such as Wellesley and Smith as well as at larger universities, where they are now common. Though women's studies itself is certainly a legitimate field of inquiry, many programs originated with strong agendas.

One author suggested that some women's studies programs should publish the following warning label as an honest expression of their intent:

> We will help your daughter discover the extent to which she has been in complicity with the patriarchy. We will encourage her to restructure herself through dialogue with us. She may become enraged and chronically offended. She will very likely reject the religious and moral codes you raised her with. She may well distance herself from family and friends. She may change her appearance, and even her sexual orientation. She may end up hating you (her father) and pitying you (her mother). After she has completed her reeducation with us, you will certainly be out tens of thousands of dollars and very possibly be out one daughter as well.[7]

Some brands of radical feminism certainly come across that way. In other words, men are the problem behind everything.

USA Today cited a study spanning the '70s, '80s, and '90s that examined how women's values had changed over time.[8] In 1920, only one out of every five women worked outside the home. By 1990, between 75 and 80 percent did. But something happened in the 1980s. Women in the survey felt that they had two full-time jobs—one outside the home and one at home, with no time for pursuing other personal interests or relationships. Juggling a career and motherhood was perhaps manageable for some, but most found it overwhelmingly stressful.

Contrasting the world of 1920 to today, violence is up, divorce is up, test scores are down, teen suicide is up, and depression is up. Many of these trends can be traced to the absence of fathers in the home, but the unavailability of mothers and the breakdown of traditional family models are contributing factors. Women felt liberated for a time and in many ways still do, and much worthwhile progress has been made. But side effects have accompanied that progress, and not all of them are good.

We have seen how the changing definitions of family have led to the disintegration of this foundational social unit. Incomes have risen dramatically for men and women as both genders have sought multiple jobs and higher pay, and some families have ended up with two, three, or even four incomes. But that comes at a cost.

Parents with such strong career-oriented drives have little time left over for parenting. And as we have seen, research shows that 80 percent of a child's personality—moral values and sense of identity—are formed in his or her first six to eight years. Too many children have been entrusted to caretakers outside the family at early ages because cultural trends have brainwashed women into believing they are not valuable unless they have a certain career or earn a certain income. Despite wonderful exceptions of believers living out their faith in family life, the culture of our day is characterized by kids who are under-nurtured, confused, and prone to depression and addiction.

Is It Better or Worse Now?

Let me be absolutely clear that the inequalities of the past had to change. Feminism has accomplished a great deal in establishing justice and equality for women. But the extreme positions and the blaming that radical feminism encourages have had destructive effects, and they compel us to ask a fundamental question: Are women's lives, marriages, and families better in the aftermath of all our politically correct experiments, or are they worse?

To answer that question, I think we have to address the core issue: What kind of life will actually lead to a woman's maximum fulfillment? Women would address that issue in a variety of different ways, and a successful career may well be the right choice for some. But if we're looking for God's design in the marriage relationship, we need to explore what embracing biblical femininity looks like and to address questions of how much energy a wife and mother needs to devote to her marriage and family.

God's blueprint leaves plenty of room for options, but it also gives us the key to making marriages work and being good parents. He has created us with certain needs that can only be satisfied in certain ways, and the only way to reach our full potential and find ultimate fulfillment is to honor his design.

God's Design for Wives

How does God define womanhood in our marriages and homes? His design has not changed along with our cultural trends; it does not go up and down, rising and falling with every movement or study or philosophy. I think we can acknowledge that as much as biblical masculinity has been distorted throughout human history, biblical femininity has been distorted even more.

The idea of womanhood has been twisted and abused and turned against the very people it should honor. That has been true from ancient times until today, though the abuses have taken various forms at various times. But we have to acknowledge that today's culture is hardly any better at defining womanhood than past cultures have been because families are disintegrating, divorces are commonplace, children are confused, and the social consequences related to the breakdown of the family—addictions, poverty, and crime, to name a few—are still a huge problem. We have missed God's design for deep, intimate marriages that are satisfying to both partners, that create homes where love and security flourish, and that remain stable over time.

We have explored God's design for womanhood and how women fit into the dance of marriage God has choreographed for our maximum fulfillment, but in no way am I trying to turn back the clock to a time when women were controlled by men and confined to the home with few options of their own.

We can point to Scripture and say that it contains the key to understanding how God created us as men and women.

We cannot point to any era in the past and say that was when things were done right. What we can do is point to Scripture and say that it contains the key to understanding how God created us as men and women, and that his plan for women is far better than any definition society has given us in the past.

So what does it look like for a wife to submit to her husband in a biblical marriage?

Early in our marriage, one of my less than loving behaviors was causing regular conflict between Theresa and me. Because I was working and going to school full-time, I felt entitled to a little pickup basketball after work. Sometimes, if I would get on a good team, we would keep winning—and if you win, you get to keep playing. I would lose all track of time, would not call Theresa, and would arrive home after our family supper.

She was understanding until it became a regular occurrence. When my apologies and promises to change (or at least call) were followed by the same habitual behavior, it became a source of constant conflict in our marriage. In my mind, I was entitled to a little fun and she was being unreasonable. In reality, I was habitually insensitive, defensive when confronted with my behavior, and unwilling to change.

The results were predictable. Theresa and I would have a fight. She wouldn't talk to me for two days, we would roll opposite ways in bed, I'd stuff my anger, she would be cold and unaffectionate, and I would quote verses to her about what a wife is supposed to do.

This became a chronic issue. I learned quickly that a good offense is better than a bad defense, so sometimes when I came home late, I would find something wrong and get on her about it right away before she had a chance to condemn me for missing supper. Yeah, we had some pretty dysfunctional ways of dealing with conflict, but we were young and didn't know any better.

I still remember the turning point. It was when Theresa applied this principle of a submissive spirit. I came in from playing basketball (late as usual). There were two candles on the table and I was waiting for the backlash. I knew the routine. But this time it was different.

She said, "If you want to sit down, your food is in the oven. I kept it warm for you." There was no hint of anger in her voice.

It felt like a trap, but I didn't say anything. I just began eating.

"Do you like it? I hope so. I worked all day. I just had thoughts of how much I love you, and I spent all day making this meal for you because I really wanted to communicate how much I care about you."

Part of me wanted her to step up and fight, because deep down I knew I was wrong. But it felt way better than our usual fight. So I kept eating as the candles burned about halfway down, and she kept saying kind and loving things. She calmly addressed the situation.

"I know we have our differences. But I feel deeply hurt when I spend all day doing something to express my love for you and then you just miss it. It feels like you don't love me."

That was like a dagger in my heart. I had never made the connection between our meals and her love for me. Not once. I had only thought about my rights, my time, and my need to work out. And she had only nagged me about her expectations, which always led to a fight.

Now, her willingness to love me and share her hurt with a submissive, tender spirit made me see the imbalance and gave her the opportunity to express her feelings in a way I understood. In that moment, with tears in my eyes, I looked at her and realized that if these meals meant love, I would be there for them. When I saw that I was hurting her, which I would never want to do on purpose, I made a decision. She changed my heart.

The way she got through to me was not by insisting that I see things her way but by doing what God said. When you relate to your husband with a gentle and submissive spirit, there is power. By contrast, when a woman sounds more like a mother than a wife with words like, "You ought . . . you should . . . you always . . . you never . . . ," men respond poorly.

> *When you relate to your husband with a gentle and submissive spirit, there is power.*

Nothing good happens when grown men hear their wives talking to them like their mothers did. (That works both ways, by the way; no woman wants to hear her husband telling her what to do like a father would.) That's a certain recipe for all kinds of problems, especially with regard to intimacy and sex. It creates a dynamic that alienates and deepens the conflict.

Theresa's attitude spoke to my heart and accomplished something that nagging or complaining never could. It was her greatest ally in bringing about the change she wanted.

What Submission Does *Not* Mean

Because the idea of submission comes with so much baggage, many people attach negative meanings to it that just aren't there in the biblical context. In the last section, we discussed what submission does mean, but I also want to caution you about what it does not mean.

It does not mean you are to be passive or feel inferior.

Submission does not imply being stepped on. Being a doormat is not God's design for your life; that isn't in his blueprint.

My wife at times gives people the impression that she is very sweet and agreeable, and she is. But there is a strength underneath that not everyone sees. When we have a disagreement, she brings it. She is respectful, but she is strong and powerful. She has deep convictions and important opinions and presents them in a calm but persuasive manner. She does not say, "Whatever you think, dear." She brings up her objections, points out my contradictions, and does a great job of expressing her thoughts and reasoning. Her submission comes after we have hashed out a lot of details and thoroughly talked through an issue. There is nothing passive about her approach, yet it is solidly biblical and it works. A good leader wants his wife to bring her strengths, thoughts, gifts, and even her best arguments to the table.

> *A good leader wants his wife to bring her strengths, thoughts, gifts, and even her best arguments to the table.*

It does not mean submitting only when you think he is right.

Submission is not the same as agreement. The test of submission is when you think to yourself, *This may be one of the dumbest things he has ever done. I've made my case, laid out the evidence, passionately argued, and he still thinks he is right and that this is what God wants him to do.* Are you still on board then? That's submission.

And all you can do in that situation is ask God to protect you both from bad mistakes and to work all things together for good, which he has already promised to do anyway.

I remember making a decision that Theresa disagreed with. It wasn't necessarily the wrong decision, but the way I did it and the timing of it was not wise. Theresa said, "I will go with you because the Bible commands me, and I will choose to have a good attitude. But I don't want to, and I don't think it's wise. In fact, I think it's pretty unwise. Nevertheless, I'm with you."

As it turns out, it *was* a dumb idea, and we paid a pretty big price for it. Graciously, Theresa never said, "I told you so." She gave me room to grow, learn, and continue to lead.

It does not mean you violate Scripture, reason, or morality to support your husband.

If your husband is leading you to lie, cheat, be unethical, be immoral, or anything else that clearly violates godly character, you submit to God and his Word rather than to your husband.

Some men come up with some pretty bizarre ideas and insist that their wives follow their leadership, but there is a difference between following your husband's bad idea and following his sinfulness. The percentage of adult Christian men who regularly view pornography has in some research topped 50 percent.[9] It would be logical to assume that these men, if married, might increasingly view their wives as an object to satisfy their lust—rather than a precious partner to cherish. Like Abigail in the Old Testament who wisely and strongly opposed her carnal and evil husband Nabal, wives at times must strongly stand against any kind of abuse or behavior that is demeaning or unwanted in the sexual relationship. First and foremost, you submit to a higher authority. If God has forbidden something, you should not let your husband lead you into it.

It does not mean you use submission as a tool to get your way.

It is possible to fake submission for a time in order to get your way in the end. I've had more than a few men share with me over the years that their wives can be really sweet and submissive at times only to discover their hidden agenda that involved remodeling the kitchen or changing their husbands' minds about a previous roadblock. (Men, of course, are guilty of the same false servanthood and leadership to get what they want.) Submission is not a tool to get your way. In fact, it has much less to do with your relationship with your husband than it does with your relationship with your heavenly Father.

Bringing It Home: Now What?

For better or worse, women, like men, are in many ways the product of their environment. The primary role model for a girl is her mom. You may have had an amazing, kind, godly mother who had wonderful priorities. She may have been a stay-at-home mom or one like mine who worked and still had the energy to be emotionally available, supervise the household, and be the glue for meals, family activities, vacations, and conflict resolution.

I would encourage you to take a minute to list the top four or five qualities you most admire about your mother. You might also list two or three things you don't want to emulate. My point is simply to get you to think about what you have consciously and unconsciously picked up from your family of origin with regard to the roles of being a woman, wife, and mother.

On the other hand, your mother may not have been around or available as often as you would have liked, or she may have been emotionally distant, preoccupied with her own issues, or focused on her work or a husband other than your father. Family life has become very messy in recent times, and the increasing number of divorces and blended families has created significant confusion for young and not-so-young women as they work through their identities. In confusing or unusual situations, how can a woman grow into the kind of woman described in Ephesians 5?

Tools for Becoming an Ephesians 5 Woman

The tools listed at the end of chapter 3 for becoming an Ephesians 5 man—*The Daily Walk Bible*, *The Five Love Languages*, and *True Spirituality* (on the kind of discipleship described in Romans 12)—are just as relevant for women. Wives will find that these resources can revolutionize the ways they relate to their husband. The following tools and practices are recommended by Theresa. They've proven to be extremely helpful to women in their spiritual and relational journey.

- Read and meditate on God's Word. Scripture promotes its own role in your life again and again: "Your word is a lamp for my feet, a light on my path" (Ps. 119:105); "You are my refuge and my shield; I have put my hope in your word" (Ps. 119:114). Many other verses declare the benefits of immersing yourself in biblical truth. Whether you use a tool like *The Daily Walk Bible* or another Bible or reading plan, the daily practice of reminding yourself of truth is life-changing. Make it a priority.

- Barbara Mouser's *Five Aspects of Woman*, an in-depth study on biblical femininity. It can help reorient your perspective to understand God's design and resist the distorted messages about femininity in today's culture.

- Affirmation cards from the series that Theresa taught entitled "Precious in His Sight." These principles provide the foundation of a positive, biblical self image. (livingontheedge.org/marriagethatworksresources)

- Here are three other regular practices that will help you become the woman God designed you to be:

  (a) Join with other women to study God's Word and pray for one another.

  (b) Pray for your husband daily.

(c) Pray for yourself. Ask according to Proverbs 31:12 that you would bring your husband good, not harm, all the days of your life.

Up to now, we've talked a lot about the roles of men and women in the marriage dance and what each partner is supposed to do. But knowing what to do and how to do it are two different things. In the remaining chapters, we are going to dive deeper into the "how" and develop a picture of what the choreography of this dance looks like in practical terms. We will move from the big picture to the real-life application—and a more fulfilling marriage and family life.

———— Questions for Reflection and Discussion ————

1. In what ways do you think traditional definitions of womanhood have fallen short? In what ways do you think modern definitions of womanhood have fallen short?

2. What are some of the challenges women face in modern Western culture?

3. If you are a woman, in what ways have you experienced tension between the desires for career and family? How have you balanced those desires?

4. How would you answer the fundamental question of whether women's lives are better because of the "politically correct" experiments of recent times?

6

What's a Man to Do?

Imagine being one of several men chosen for a critical mission. Part of your preparation means entering US Marines special-ops training. It's a nine-month course, and on day one, the commander introduces the program.

"Men," he says, "you are about to go through the most difficult training of your life. Your commitment to stay on track and have each other's back will determine whether you live or die. If you are successful, you will save tens of thousands of lives. If not, you will die. So will those tens of thousands of lives."

The pressure is on. It's time to step up. Envision it: treading water for an hour nonstop with clothes and boots on, running twelve miles carrying forty-five pounds of gear, being dropped into extreme conditions that demand survival skills, mastering battle and marksmanship skills, and more. You and your band of brothers have to make quick decisions, keep your commitments, and stretch yourself far harder and deeper than you ever thought you could go. But in the process, you will change the world.

A God-Centered Worldview

That's the spirit in which Moses pulled together the next generation of leaders after enduring a forty-year trek through the wilderness and watching many of his companions fail. Many died out of disobedience. They thus did not fulfill the mission or keep their commitment.

So in his last words to the assembled tribes of Israel, Moses spoke bluntly to their leaders, their men. He reminded them of the commandments God had given and how those decrees were to be instilled in their children and their children's children. He described what it means to fear God and how God rewards obedience with long life and fruitfulness.

These instructions would be essential to remember because the people of Israel would be entering a land filled with diverse gods and goddesses, blatant idolatry, and rampant perversion. So Moses assured the people that there was only one God, and this God's desire for his people was all-encompassing: "Love the LORD your God with all your heart and with all your soul and with all your strength" (Deut. 6:5).

Then he gave them a picture of what that kind of devotion should look like. They were to teach God's ways to their children, formally and informally—to provide instruction and then to impress it on their hearts by talking about it when they got up, when they lay down, and when they went about their business.

Far more than giving them information, God, through Moses, was giving his people a worldview to shape their lives. Why? So he could bless and prosper them as expressions of his love.

The temptations in the land of prosperity would be great; the human heart tends to drift away in times of abundance. But there would be consequences because God is jealous for the love of his people. To bring them back, he would allow them to experience hardships that would make a Marine's special-ops training look like a walk in the park.

Your God-Given Assignment

That scenario in Deuteronomy, when Moses was preparing the people for the special mission of entering into the Promised Land and serving God faithfully, highlights principles that are extremely relevant for us today, especially for men as leaders in their homes. In this chapter, we are going to explore what God wants men to do. We have already looked at a description of the role and discussed what it means to *be* a real man, but here we learn what a man is to *do*—his responsibilities.

Men, you need to know that your God-given assignment can be extremely rewarding but also pretty intense. It requires commitment, and you can't do it alone. You may not have many role models to look at for inspiration; not many of us do. I got the Marine part of a father, not the Christian part, as I was growing up. But if you are willing to embrace a picture different from what our culture teaches, you will be richly rewarded.

> *Men, you need to know that your God-given assignment can be extremely rewarding but also pretty intense.*

You will become the kind of man who attracts the kind of woman you dream about and helps her grow into the woman of your dreams. You will become the kind of man that your sons want to emulate and your daughters want to marry. You will learn to walk with the integrity and character that reflects the nature of God and prepares you to receive his best for your life.

Show Me the Box Top

I have a friend near Lake Tahoe who often lets me get away to his A-frame house to spend some time with family or to focus on study. Once when I was visiting him there, I walked in to see a coffee table covered with a beautiful picture. I looked a little closer and realized it was made up of thousands of separate pieces that had come out of a box sitting nearby.

I have never been very good at puzzles. "If my life depended on it," I told him, "I could never do something like that."

"Oh no, Chip, you really could," he assured me. "Here's the key. You just have to have the box top. If you can see the picture, all you need to do is take it a step at a time."

He walked me through his process of finding all the border pieces, then grouping the remaining pieces by color and piecing them together bit by bit. "If you do it little by little, have a lot of patience, and realize it's a journey, you could put that whole thing together yourself. It all depends on looking at the box top."

That's exactly the advice I want to give men in this chapter. You are going to get the biblical equivalent of a special-ops Marine box top in the next few pages—the job description Scripture gives you for being a man, a husband, and a father.

If you look at it as a to-do list or something you need to accomplish in a few weeks, you will lose heart and give up. But if you see it as a pathway, a journey toward being the man you were created to be, with a marriage and a life you were created to have, you will grow into the picture you see. You will become what you envision, and in that transformation you will make a difference in your home, your work, your neighborhood, and everywhere you have influence. You will fulfill your mission.

My father did the best he could, given his life experiences. I've told you a little of his story—how he struggled with alcoholism and his memories of the war, and how he came to Christ at the age of fifty-five. His dad died when he was thirteen, so he didn't have a clear picture of fatherhood to grow into, and he didn't know how to give me a clear picture either. So when I married Theresa, who had been abandoned shortly after her twin boys were born, I was immediately a husband and father of four-year-olds at the same time; and I had no idea how to fulfill either of those roles.

I have been in special-ops training for more than three decades to progressively become the kind of man that my sons would want to be like, that my daughter would want to marry, and that my wife would want to tell her friends about. They are all aware of my flaws and know I have a lot of growing to do, but I want them to see the heart of God in my love for them. And I want them to pass that same heart down to future generations.

Finding the Right Picture

Knowing your role as a husband is one thing; living it out is another. What exactly are you supposed to do? What does your leadership look like in your marriage and your home? What does it mean to step up in love? What do real men do?

Society does not give us the right box top for this puzzle. We get all sorts of images of manhood, but as we have seen, most are unreliable, and even the good examples are often mixed with distorted elements. We get pieces of the puzzle, but we need the picture on the top of the box to show us how to put it together.

> *Knowing your role as a husband is one thing; living it out is another.*

You have entered into the dance, which we discussed in chapter 2. You have stepped up in love. What does that look like for a real man? Scripture tells us that you need to provide, protect, and nurture.

That covers a lot of territory. Most of us men understand the financial-provision part of this instruction, but we tend to struggle more with the spiritual and emotional parts. But the biblical picture covers all of it.

This is a comprehensive calling into manhood, and it flows out of sacrificial love as demonstrated by Christ's love for the church and depicted in Ephesians 5. We are going to look at these three specific areas—providing, protecting, and nurturing—through the lens of some other verses of Scripture that fill out the picture for us. What we're going to see is that the New Testament version of being a nonconformist, like the picture Moses gave the Israelites in Deuteronomy, requires a heart commitment and skills that can change the course of a whole family's destiny.

We'll continue our discussion of a man's responsibility in the following three chapters, each with questions and resources to help you digest and think through the implications of God's design for you in your marriage.

7

Stepping Up as a Man: *Provide*

As a man, you are to provide financially for your family. That does not mean that your wife must always stay at home and never have a job. It also does not mean that you are less of a man if you go through a period of unemployment or struggle in your path toward financial security.

It does mean, however, that the burden of responsibility for providing for the physical needs of your wife and children, of making sure the bills get paid, and of staying out of unreasonable or unwise debt is on your shoulders.

"But if anyone does not provide for his own, and especially for those of his household, he has denied the faith and is worse than an unbeliever" (1 Tim. 5:8 NASB). The translation of that verse is that the welfare of the home is the man's moral responsibility.

You are the family's chief financial officer, the CFO. If the numbers don't add up, you can't blame the accountants. You're the man. If there is not enough money to go around or if your debt ratio gets too high, it will be on your shoulders, and you will be the one who has to address the underlying issues and implement changes.

Your wife can certainly help out, but there may be times when her family responsibilities don't allow her to earn income. Your job is to take the pressure off her and declare that you own the moral responsibility to provide food, shelter, and clothing not only now but also in the future.

Please don't translate the last paragraph to mean you're all alone in this or that you need to make all the decisions or handle all the finances; what we're talking about is who holds the moral weight and responsibility for the finances. As I outline the five major financial objectives for your finances, know there are a number of practical ways to accomplish these that will vary from family to family based on skill and giftedness.

Five Financial Objectives

The following five specific objectives go along with financial responsibility:

1. Do honest work.
2. Honor God first.
3. Live within your means.

4. Prepare for the future.

5. Train your children.

1. Do honest work.

The first objective starts with you. Your wife and children need to see your example of what it means to work hard and work well, with diligence and integrity. No shortcuts, no cheating. "Whatever you do, work at it with all your heart, as working for the Lord, not for human masters" (Col. 3:23).

When you apply diligence and integrity to your career responsibilities as well as household tasks, you are setting an example of someone working primarily for the Lord rather than human beings. In a very real sense, your work is ultimately an act of worship. One of the greatest gifts you can pass on to your children is a strong, clear work ethic. It will change their lives. So do your work with excellence.

> *In a very real sense, your work is ultimately an act of worship.*

2. Honor God first.

You are the steward of your finances. You may get a paycheck once a week, twice a month, once a month, or only on commission. However it looks for you, your income came from the hand of God before it passed through the hands of your employer or your clients. You are the manager of his money, the steward of whatever he has entrusted to you. You need to live and handle money and possessions with that mindset.

The clearest way to maintain that stewardship mindset is to give your first and best back to him. When you do, you make a statement that he is the one in control and that you trust him.

In the Old Testament, the first and best was usually the pick of your livestock or the first of your harvest. In a money economy, that became a 10 percent tithe—not an afterthought after all the bills are paid, but right off the top. That number is not a maximum and it's not a legalist "bill" to pay. It's a statement of faith and step of obedience; as you get older and your income increases, you can increase your percentage to give even more. And yes, in times of financial crisis, God may give you different specifics to be able to honor him while still making ends meet.

But in general, this is a foundational way that you express your love and trust to the One who has provided you with the means to earn a living and support your family. You are the CFO of your family, but God is the CEO of the universe, and his blessing comes to those who trust him. It takes a step of faith to model that perspective for your wife and children. And God promises to provide for your needs (Phil. 4:19) and bless your life in ways far beyond money (Luke 6:38).

3. Live within your means.

Make sure you have more money coming in than going out. That may make things really tight sometimes, and that's okay. Most families look back on lean times with fondness because they know they accomplished something difficult together.

The alternative is much worse. Indebtedness can enslave you. At the very least, it limits your freedom later. The average college student is $28,950 in debt;[1] many of them file for bankruptcy before they ever start their careers. They have learned from their parents and their culture that debt is a way of life, and they have not yet learned to discipline themselves. Because of their debts, many young adults are not able to follow God's leading into careers like ministry and missions, or they are forced to delay marriage or begin family life with extraordinary financial pressure. Their debt has taken their freedom. Fathers are strategy number one for preventing that tragedy, and it begins by modeling for the family how to live within your means.

I made my way through seminary by selling insurance and investments. I regularly met people who made six- and seven-figure incomes but had cash-flow problems. The issue was never their amount of income; it was discipline in managing their expenses and lifestyle choices. Most people figure out how to spend their income easily, and then they stretch beyond it just a little bit. Pretty soon, they are wrestling with overwhelming debt, even though their income was good to begin with.

We live in a culture that teaches us to buy now and pay later. As the financial managers of our families, we have to set the pace and go against the trends of the culture. Real men, godly men, live within their means.

4. Prepare for the future.

I've read that the average American today saves only around 2 percent of his or her income, and many don't save anything at all.[2] The days when most families saved for the future are gone. You need to have a savings plan, even if you start with what seems like an insignificant amount. When Theresa and I started saving, we had three kids and I was making only $1,800 a month as pastor of a tiny church. But we put away $50 each month for retirement. Developing the practice and the discipline is far more important than the amount.

In addition, you really do need to have a will. You need life insurance. Someone needs to know where your savings and investments are. You may need a financial planner to help. Perhaps you expect to live a long life (I hope you do!), but the majority of Christian men have not made provisions for their families in case of their deaths. It's one of those things we keep procrastinating on that just has to get done. Preparing for your family's future with or without you is your moral responsibility as leader of your home.

5. Train your children.

Many faith-based financial trainers have taught us about the beauty of compound interest. They recommend a simple formula to help our children learn the basics of financial management. It's the 10/10/80 principle: give the first 10 percent to the Lord, save the next 10 percent, and live on the last 80 percent.

If we as adults modeled this basic plan and taught our children the same, we would avoid some of life's biggest problems. Most, though, have not been taught to do this (see point 3, "Live within your means"). Marriages end over issues like this. Many people get divorced not because they stop loving each other but because they don't have enough money and start arguing about whose fault it is.

But when we step up as men and put our family's financial security on our shoulders, we change the destructive patterns that many in our society never overcome. It can be extremely difficult at first, and it may have to begin with very small steps. That was certainly true for me, but the payoff has been way beyond the pain. Looking at how my grown children handle their money and the pitfalls they missed because of that make all the challenges seem minor today.

It's easy to get caught up in the details of what to do and what not to do as you live out these objectives, so I want to turn our focus to the core values behind them. Being a man is not a legalistic list of details to remember; it's an expression of who you really are and what you really believe—the true you God designed you to be. It's about letting Christ transform your nature and then living out of your true identity.

The objectives I've listed will help you get started and measure your progress, but they are simply the outcomes of the core values you embrace. Let's take a deeper look at the root of these objectives.

Your Core Values as Provider

One of those values is a Christlike work ethic. Beyond just owning this value for yourself as you approach your work, it is critical for you to instill it in your children. Theresa and I started when our children were very young.

We showed them how to make the bed and take out the garbage. When they got older, we let them help out with cooking, dishes, and laundry. We gave them an alarm clock so they would learn to get themselves up and ready for school.

Feed your children more responsibility, in appropriate measures, so they become more independent from you and more dependent on God. Yes, it takes time and it's far easier to just do things for them. But it's in this process that they form positive habits and gain confidence and strong self-worth. As you live out the work ethic you want your children to emulate, you're preparing them for success in whatever God calls them to do.

Another core value is stewardship of time and money. This means more than giving a portion of income. It is a mindset, an attitude, a biblical worldview that you're seeking to help your children develop. We began teaching our kids the 10/10/80 principle when they were about two years old. We put three jars on each of their dressers. Each had a label: one said "Giving"; another, "Saving"; and the third, "Spending."

> *Feed your children more responsibility, in appropriate measures, so they become more independent from you and more dependent on God.*

Early on, they would get ten pennies for picking up their toys or doing some other basic task, then we increased it to dimes, quarters, and dollars as they grew. It was a visual picture of how they would eventually structure their budgets as adults. They learned that everything belongs to God and that there were always opportunities to be generous—with a visiting missionary, a sponsored child whose picture we put on our re-frigerator, a fund-raising drive, or the church offering plate. They also learned that the longer they saved, the more they could buy—the gift of delayed gratification. If they wanted to splurge on something like designer jeans or expensive sneakers, we would contribute what we would have spent on normal jeans or shoes and let them earn the rest. We set the pace for them to follow.

How you use money is just a symptom of a mindset, but it reflects your true values. It is a good indication of how you view your stewardship. You have to be a little more creative to teach your children how to manage their time, but the principle is the same: it all comes from God, and we want to learn, and we have to be responsible in how we use it.

Jesus talked more about money than about heaven and hell combined, not because God needs our money but because our hearts will be wherever our treasure is. He also talked about time—using it wisely to be fruit-ful and be ready for his return—because that's a reflection of our values too. It is a matter of stewardship, of responsibil-ity, and of personal discipline. These are challenging things to practice, let alone teach our kids, but they are important issues in God's economy. And as a man, it's my responsibility to make them important issues at home.

> *How you use money is just a symptom of a mindset, but it reflects your true values.*

Finally, stewardship isn't all about discipline and self-denial. God actually commands us to celebrate and enjoy the good gifts he brings into our lives. Paul warns against putting too much hope in riches, but he also tells us that God gives all things for us richly to enjoy (1 Tim. 6:17). Sometimes you need to go out for an amazing meal or have a great vacation. Plan for those things, and don't go into debt for them. But don't be afraid to enjoy the gifts God has given you. Live with joy and generosity, and your children will grow up with a healthy understanding of the goodness of God.

> God actually commands us to celebrate and enjoy the good gifts he brings into our lives.

There's a lot to process here. Let me encourage you to willfully set aside some time to let this content sink in. I've developed some questions and resources to help you with that.

Questions for Reflection and Discussion

1. What was most helpful in this chapter for you? Why?

2. Which of the five practices discussed in this chapter do you find come most naturally to you?

3. Which of the five practices do you sense needs some additional attention or focus from you? Why?

4. What's the biggest barrier or challenge you are facing in providing for your wife? Your family?

5. Who could help you take those next steps to provide for your family the way you want and need to?

Recommended Resources

Master Your Money, by Ron Blue

The Treasure Principle, by Randy Alcorn

Sermon audio, book, and Bible study: "The Genius of Generosity," by Chip Ingram (livingontheedge.org/marriagethatworksresources)

Sermon audio and Bible study: "Balancing Life's Demands" by Chip Ingram. This series unpacks how to develop biblical priorities with your finances and time. (livingontheedge.org/marriagethatworksresources)

Sermon audio: "Download—Passing On What Matters Most," by Chip Ingram. (livingontheedge.org/marriagethatworksresources)

8

Stepping Up as a Man: *Protect*

Many men see financial and material provision as their primary, or *only*, responsibility in the home. But husbands also hold the crucial responsibility for the spiritual development and protection of their families. In essence, you are not only the family's CFO, you are also the spiritual leader.

That is not how it works in most homes; women often find themselves providing the spiritual direction for their husbands and children to follow. But God has appointed us as men to take responsibility for the spiritual welfare of our families.

That does not mean fathers do everything for their families spiritually. Each member has his or her own relationship with God. But a man who serves as the spiritual leader for his family will take his wife's needs, hurts, fears, and struggles to God on her behalf and ask for wisdom and guidance to provide spiritual direction and encouragement to his wife. I actually pictured myself as a family priest: one who brings God's Word and heart to my family and my family's needs to Christ. If that sounds above your paygrade and you think there's no way you could ever do that, hang in there—I felt the same way, but little by little, God helped me take baby steps that eventually transformed our marriage and our family. Here are what I think are the five top objectives to get you started.

Five Spiritual Objectives

As with your financial responsibilities, your spiritual responsibilities come with five practical objectives:

1. Set the pace personally.

2. Know the spiritual condition of your wife and children.

3. Pray for and with your wife and children regularly.

4. Ensure that biblical instruction takes place at home and at church.

5. Make experiencing God and loving each other your top priority.

1. Set the pace personally.

Your family will follow your example. It's improbable that your children will grow up to love God's Word unless they see their father loving his Word. They are not likely to grow up praying with passion unless they see you praying that way. (This applies to many areas of life, not just the spiritual ones, like it or not. They drive the way you drive, talk the way you talk, and respond to setbacks the way you do. They watch, and they learn by example.) Jesus said it best: "The student is not above the teacher, but everyone who is fully trained will be like their teacher" (Luke 6:40).

That does not mean you have to be perfect. It means that when you mess up, they need to see a healthy response—admitting your flaws, apologizing for your mistakes, and learning from them. When I've blown it with Theresa, my kids need to see me apologize. When I

> *As husbands and fathers, we need to model following God's will and repenting for missing it.*

exaggerate something from the pulpit—it doesn't happen often, but sometimes a story takes on a life of its own—they need me to acknowledge that "it didn't actually happen like that."

As husbands and fathers, we need to model following God's will and repenting for missing it. We set the pace for our wives and children.

2. Know the spiritual condition of your wife and children.

One of the biggest mistakes I've made as a husband and father is assuming everything is okay because it seemed so by outward appearance. The old adage that "men are insensitive" really applied to me. I discovered the hard way that I needed to become a student of my wife to learn how she thinks, what her weaknesses are, and where she struggles so

I can relate to her with understanding and let the grace of God in me help her grow and develop. "Husbands, in the same way be considerate as you live with your wives, and treat them with respect as the weaker partner and as heirs with you of the gracious gift of life, so that nothing will hinder your prayers" (1 Pet. 3:7).

Sometimes we have to ask our wives, "How are you really doing?" and be prepared to really listen, not to try to fix whatever we hear.

The process works the same way with our children. Staying in tune with what they are struggling with is critical. One of my sons went through a period of struggling with pornography, even though he really had a heart for following God and had always been diligent about reading his Bible and talking to his friends about his faith.

As spiritual leader of my family, it was my job to walk with him through that difficult experience—first to know him well enough to notice the signs, then to ask him the right questions and talk honestly about the problem, and then to help him get free from it. It was a painful and uncomfortable situation, but avoiding issues like that sets the wrong spiritual tone. When my son later went to college, he was able to help many of his friends who were struggling with the same issue. Learning to step up as a spiritual leader sets the direction of your family and bears fruit in their lives for years to come.

Sometimes you will have to say no. When your daughter is dating a guy who acts nice but seems to have another side to his personality, when your child's friends are rubbing off on them in negative ways, when your kids develop unhealthy habits or pursue unwholesome activities . . . your job is to intervene.

Many parents are afraid of saying no because they don't want their kids to rebel. As a dad, you can't afford to focus on your own reputation with your kids, though doing the right thing will probably earn their respect in the long run. It is still your responsibility to do the right thing, even if they say they hate you in the moment. If your kids' hearts get attached to the wrong people or the wrong behaviors, you are going to lose them.

A spiritual leader is willing to confront, to risk favor in the short term in order to accomplish a long-term good. That's what love does.

3. Pray for and with your wife and children regularly.

Use meals, bedtimes, informal conversations in the car, and every other opportunity to center the lives of your family members on God. Lift them up constantly to God. Zealously guard the spiritual life of your family not only through your leadership but also in your prayers.

4. Ensure that biblical instruction takes place at home and at church.

Use those same meals, bedtimes, and informal conversations to bring biblical instruction to your family's hearts and minds. You don't have to do that alone; it should be a group experience, and your church is part of that equation.

But if your kids are not getting biblical instruction, it's your job to make sure they do. If your wife is struggling in her spiritual life, you are the one to walk her through it. When I stand before God one day, he is not going to ask me how well a church or Christian school guided my family. He is going to ask me how well *I* did. In reality, your wife and children will benefit from a variety of spiritual influences, and your church will be one of the biggest ones. But the primary responsibility for creating the right environment is yours.

5. Make experiencing God and loving each other your top priority.

Your aim is not morality. That's an outcome, not the main focus. Otherwise, you will end up being a legalistic (and probably very boring) husband and father who doesn't realize how easily the rest of the family tunes you out. Strict religious talk does not win hearts or change lives. A real relationship with God and genuine love between family members are a powerful combination. Superficial dos and don'ts are not. Your family needs life, love, joy, and authentic experience. When they see this in your life, it spills over into theirs.

> *Your family needs life, love, joy, and authentic experience. When they see this in your life, it spills over into theirs.*

Our family made it a habit to go out together after our Ssaturday night service and have a good time. They would "criticize" my messages—in a constructive way—and let me know which parts were boring and help me rewrite my notes for Sunday's services. I still remember how precious taking my daughter out for breakfast on Sunday mornings was for both of us. Even as a preteen, she would help me with my messages. She could point out all my failed attempts to talk about teenagers in their language and give me the right words. We would eat together, laugh, sing along with the radio on the way home, and have a great time.

I never wanted my family to experience a stuffy, religious home. I wanted them to know their opinions mattered, their views and experiences were important, and that part of following God is having a full and fun life.

Your Core Values as Protector

As in our discussion of financial responsibilities, behind each of these spiritual objectives are some critical core values. The details are far less important than the values you hold. In fulfilling your spiritual responsibilities toward your wife and children, you want to do more than check all the boxes. You want to live in dependency on God, evidenced by prayer and even fasting when necessary; to embody faith in God and his Word; to have a service and outreach orientation; to be outwardly focused; and to experience progressive growth in holiness.

> *In fulfilling your spiritual responsibilities toward your wife and children, you want to do more than check all the boxes.*

I think one of the best expressions of these values is in Philippians 4:8: "Whatever is true, whatever is noble, whatever is right, whatever is pure, whatever is lovely, whatever is admirable—if anything is excellent or praiseworthy—think about such things."

One of the most challenging obstacles to living out the core value of protection today is guarding what comes into your home in music, videos, and games. If you don't set limits, things can easily get out of control.

You will have to be consistent in deciding what is and is not allowed in your house in terms of violence, sex, and other questionable content. It gets even more difficult when you try to set limits on the heroes your son wants to emulate or on the immodest styles your teenage daughter wants to wear. You understand the message she is unintentionally sending better than she does and probably better than her mother does. She needs her father to have a gentle, sympathetic, but honest conversation with her about the ways a teenage boy's mind works. And she always needs to know from the man in the house that she is beautiful, so she won't have to seek that affirmation elsewhere.

There's a lot of ground in this practical chapter. Don't let time go by before intentionally thinking through what we've discussed to your life today. These questions and resources can help.

Questions for Reflection and Discussion

1. What was most helpful in this chapter for you? Why?

2. Which of the five practices discussed in this chapter do you find come most naturally to you?

3. Which of the five practices do you sense needs some additional attention or focus from you? Why?

4. What's the biggest barrier or challenge you are facing in protecting your wife? Your family?

5. Who could help you take those next steps to protect your family the way you want and need to?

Recommended Resources

The Real God, by Chip Ingram

The Real God Family Devotional, by Living on the Edge (livingontheedge.org/marriagethatworksresources)

Sermon audio, book, and Bible study: "True Spirituality," by Chip Ingram (livingontheedge.org/marriagethatworksresources)

Sermon audio and Bible study: "Transformed—The Miracle of Life Change," by Chip Ingram (livingontheedge.org/marriagethatworks resources)

Sermon audio and Bible study: "Overcoming Emotions That Destroy," by Chip Ingram (livingontheedge.org/marriagethatworksresources)

Sermon audio, book, and Bible study: "Effective Parenting in a Defective World," by Chip Ingram (livingontheedge.org/marriagethatworks resources)

9

Stepping Up as a Man: *Nurture*

Husbands hold the primary responsibility for relational health, the welfare of their families. That means that in addition to being the CFO and the spiritual leader, you are also the coach.

Just as in the world of sports, the direction of your "team" depends to a large degree on the kind of coaching it gets. "If anyone does not know how to manage his own family, how can he take care of God's church?" (1 Tim. 3:5). This verse deals primarily with leaders in the church, but it assumes that men are meant to be household managers.

I am the head of the Ingram franchise; you are the head of your family franchise. Success is determined by how well the team functions with love, obedience, and respect toward God and one another. If the culture of the franchise isn't right, it's up to you to change it.

Five Relational Objectives

Again, your relational role comes with five practical objectives:

1. Verbalize and celebrate the marriage covenant.

2. Schedule time to develop marriage and family relationships.

3. Provide structure and boundaries to ensure that family relationships take priority over outside demands.

4. Build communication into the fabric and rhythm of the family schedule.

5. Implement consequences fairly, firmly, and lovingly among all family members.

1. Verbalize and celebrate the marriage covenant.

I have a friend who gathered his children together when they were all old enough to understand what divorce is and had friends whose parents had split up. He put a big dictionary on the table, pulled out a knife, opened to the word "divorce," read the definition out loud, and then cut the whole entry out of the dictionary. "In our home," he said, "we want you to know that this word is not in our vocabulary."

> Make it a goal to show outward signs of your commitment to your marriage.

Make it a goal to show outward signs of your commitment to your marriage. For example, be affectionate with your wife—even if your kids roll their eyes and tell you to get a room. Kids may think it's gross when you make it clear you still think their mom is hot. But something deep down inside them will find comfort in the fact that their relational world is stable. They need to know the honeymoon isn't over and that your life together is alive and full of love.

2. Schedule time to develop marriage and family relationships.

You know how to schedule appointments with colleagues, clients, doctors, and repairmen. Don't let your wife and children fall through the cracks of your schedule. Plan time together. Have a regular date with your wife. Determine to eat a certain number of meals together as a family each week. Work in a regular playtime or date time with your sons and daughters. Approach your task with the commitment of a Navy SEAL or Army Ranger, and find a way to fit it all in. This is one of the most important parts of your mission.

3. Provide structure and boundaries to ensure that family relationships take priority over outside demands.

You have to structure your life to make sure you allow enough room for your kids to be involved and well rounded without eating every meal on the fly. If you don't, your family life will be dictated by youth sports, music practices, academics, and all the important activities that kids will want to be involved in but may have a tendency to overdo.

Again, be the bad cop for the moment whom they will respect years down the road. Say no when they want to fit three sports into one season. You are not depriving your kids to limit their activities. You are providing a healthy home environment where relationships can strengthen and grow.

4. Build communication into the fabric and rhythm of the family schedule.

Have you ever been in the room with the rest of your family when every member is on some kind of device? Or when all your free time is taken up by TV programming rather than conversation? Put the electronics away for meals and set a time nightly when everyone (including you) signs off of email, texts, Slack, Instagram, and Facebook. Make sure you eat together regularly and make those times an occasion for regular communication. Take advantage of time in the car to talk instead of just listening to the radio or having everyone occupied with their earbuds. Build a heart connection with every member of the family.

> *Build a heart connection with every member of the family.*

5. Implement consequences fairly, firmly, and lovingly among all family members.

My kids didn't always like my efforts at discipline and setting boundaries, but I tried not to focus on how they would react in the moment. I wanted them to love me ten years down the road.

I know I made a lot of mistakes along the way, especially with one of my sons. But I recently had some father-son time with all three of them during a family vacation. We get away somewhere for a week every year with the children and grandchildren, and my three sons and I were on a porch, sitting in rocking chairs and talking. The son I had the most challenges with looked at me and said this: "Dad, there are no victims here. Even with all the things I really resented, I am who I am because of you. I chafed under some of those things, but even the ones you got wrong—and I appreciate your apologizing for them—turned out okay. God has sovereignly taken all of it, and I think about all of our lives, the women we married, the way we are raising our kids, and I know we are all in this together."

I don't know what you want to get out of life, but when you have sons and daughters who grow up still wanting to be your friend, who love God and live with integrity, it doesn't get any better than that.

I know I wasn't always a wonderful dad, but I was intent on being an authentic dad. And I think my kids recognized that their mother and I were doing our best to teach and train them, to be fair with them, and to set them up for a life of faithfulness and fruitfulness.

Your children are all unique, so you have to use different approaches with each of them. But they are all equally loved and valued, so you have to be fair. That's a hard balance, and sometimes you will get it wrong. But they will see your leadership and love for them, and they will grow up knowing their heavenly Father through their earthly one.

Your Core Values as Nurturer

The heart of all these objectives is, as always, your core values. The relational environment of your home needs to be filled with acceptance and affirmation given in the context of accountability.

You are called to be a man of God, spend time with your wife, play with your kids, and cultivate an atmosphere of love and affirmation. These things don't happen on their own. You decide to be that kind of man, you begin with specific steps (even if they are small), and you grow over time. It's a process.

> The relational environment of your home needs to be filled with acceptance and affirmation given in the context of accountability.

You will have to make some hard decisions along the way. You may have to make less money in order to give your family quality time. You may disappoint your kids by saying no right now in order to set them up for long-term success. But one of the greatest needs in our culture right now is for men to be men.

I didn't know how to do that at first. You may not either. But be encouraged by the fact that this is a journey. You are on it with other men, and you have the help of the God of the universe. In most cases, you will also have the enthusiastic support of your wife. With commitment, focus, and perseverance, you will be able to fulfill your financial, spiritual, and relational responsibilities—your roles as CFO, spiritual leader, and coach—with God's supernatural blessing and strength.

———————— Questions for Reflection and Discussion ————————

1. How would you describe your ideal family environment? In what ways are you encouraged with your role in leading your wife and family?

2. If you are a man, which leadership role do you find most challenging: financial provider, spiritual leader, or relational guide? Why?

3. In what ways do your responsibilities as a man require commitment and perseverance? Who or what helps you strengthen your commitment?

4. In what ways has this chapter helped you understand the process of creating the family dynamics you want to experience? What specific steps can you take now to move toward your goals for your marriage and family?

5. Who could you invite to join you on this journey for encouragement, strength, and accountability?

Recommended Resources

Sermon audio: "Portrait of a Father," by Chip Ingram (livingontheedge .org/marriagethatworksresources)

Sermon audio and Bible study: "Experiencing God's Dream for Your Marriage," by Chip Ingram (livingontheedge.org/marriagethatworks resources)

10

What's a Woman to Do?

picked up a women's magazine while I was standing in line at the store recently. I had noticed the cover story of a famous actress, a single woman in her forties, who decided to have a baby. She is extremely wealthy, considered one of the most beautiful women in the world, and has dated, lived with, or been married to some of the world's most popular men. By most accounts, she has reached the pinnacle of success.

In spite of that success, I felt sad for her. The article explained how she had always wanted to have a baby and thought that she would be married at this point in her life. She felt that the one thing she was missing out on in life was being able to offer motherly love.

But, as she explained, women are realizing more and more that they don't need a man to have a child—that there are many more options than there used to be. So even though it would be ideal to become a mother with a man by her side, she was tired of waiting for the right guy. She was going to rearrange her life to make motherhood a priority, and she was confident she was strong enough to do it on her own.

This woman had accomplished everything our culture says will make a person happy, yet there was still a hole in her heart, an ache for something she had missed along the way. Situations like hers are a fruit of the sexual revolution in the '60s and '70s, when sex and marriage became disconnected. Men no longer feel compelled to commit to marriage in order to have sex, and women no longer feel compelled to give devotion and sex in order to build a relationship. When the components of a marriage relationship are separated and detached from marriage, you end up with many relationships that are not lasting or fulfilling.

By her own admission, this woman had been living in fear that she would never experience some of the things she was designed by God to experience. Yet she had followed the culture's prescription for fulfillment far more successfully than most people ever do. She was a role model who was missing out on one of her biggest roles.

Show Me *Which* Box Top

Women today are given a variety of roles to fulfill, and some of them are mutually exclusive. They can't fulfill them all. While the issue for men was finding the box top—discovering the model for manhood that most men have never seen up close—the issue for women is *which* box top to look at.

Are you supposed to be like the famous actress who has beauty, wealth, and lots of men who are uncommitted? Are you supposed to be like Mother Teresa and dedicate your life to a cause that may be far removed from the life you have always known? Should you pursue a career or get married and have a family? Or try to balance both? And if both, how long should you do one before you begin the other? In other words, what is your calling? What does God want you to be and do in life?

We have already discussed the basics of a wife's role—to step in and support her husband. That's the "what." In this chapter, we will look at the "how." I have to warn you, however, that it may come across as a little controversial. In fact, just as I offered the hypothetical warning label for women's studies programs I quoted in chapter 5, I offer a similar warning:

The message you are about to hear may be hazardous to your emotional equilibrium. It may call into question assumptions and preconceived ideas you've had about womanhood, marriage, and motherhood. Though ancient in their origin and tested successfully for centuries, these concepts may sound strange, countercultural, and even bizarre to the ears of twenty-first-century men and women. The implications of this message for your life and family could be drastic, even disturbing. If applied en masse by those who claim allegiance to Jesus Christ, it could be revolutionary.

God's view of women is simultaneously liberating, countercultural, and counterintuitive—and it works.

Three Priorities

At first glance, God's prescription for your marriage and family relationships will look a lot like the husband's. As I've studied this, I've found that the wife has the same three priorities: to nurture, protect, and provide. That's because, as we have seen, the divine Designer gives us complementary roles that are neither superior nor inferior to each other. But as part of their complementary nature, the emphases are different.

The wife's three priorities are in exactly the opposite order of the husband's. The husband's first priority is to provide, then protect, then nurture. The wife's is first to nurture, then protect, then provide.

> *The husband's first priority is to provide, then protect, then nurture. The wife's is first to nurture, then protect, then provide.*

God has designed us to fit together in a way that creates unity and strength in our love and intimacy—that beautiful dance we have been talking about—and it creates a home instead of just a house. We see the same complementary nature whenever two parts fit together to work as one.

Much of my home is held together by nuts and bolts that I can't see. I see walls and floors and ceilings. But behind the visible appearance are pieces that hold everything together, and those pieces don't work by themselves. The bolt will not hold its place without the nut; the nut accomplishes nothing unless it fits around a bolt. Their threads look just alike, but they have to turn in opposite directions to fit together. It's the combination that provides the strength.

The "threads" of men and women look a lot alike, but we have to turn in opposite directions to fit together. The beauty is in the strength, and the strength comes from each person complementing or completing the other person's role.

So the divine Designer has given wives three priorities in opposite order of their husbands':

1. To *nurture* is to create a relational environment that promotes the spiritual, emotional, and physical welfare of those around you.

2. To *protect* means to minimize the harmful influences that affect the lives that have been entrusted to you.

3. To *provide* means to maximize all spiritual, emotional, physical, and financial resources to do good to those who are in your relational network.

Just as God has made husbands to step up with love and leadership to meet the needs wives cannot meet on their own, he has created wives to step in with honor and respect to meet their husbands' needs and do what they are not able to do alone. It's a role only a wife can fill, and when she does, she experiences the deepest levels of joy and fulfillment in her heart.

These priorities will shape a wife's approach to three specific roles: as champion for her husband, mother for her children, and mentor for younger women. As a woman, you know your responsibilities are more numerous than this, and the demands placed on you will reach far beyond these specific functions. You will be counselor, psychologist, medic, cook, cleaner, instructor, developer, discipler, traveler, chauffeur, and much, much more. But most of them fit into three main categories.

No one else can meet the needs of your husband, your children, and younger women in the ways you can. These are the main areas of responsibility God has gifted you to address.

Similar to our discussion of a man's responsibility, I've created three shorter chapters, each with questions and resources to help you digest and think through the implications of God's design for you in your marriage.

11

Stepping In as a Woman: *Nurture*

The three priorities God has given to wives may be expressed in different ways in the various seasons of life. Not all of them are at the forefront all the time. But they are all part of God's original design, and no one can do them like each individual wife can. The first is to be a nurturer to her husband.

At creation, God's intended role for the wife was to be a helper. "It is not good for the man to be alone," he said. "I will make a helper suitable for him" (Gen. 2:18). The word "helper," by the way, does not suggest a subordinate position. It is also used of God himself in several places in the Old Testament, such as when he was Israel's "helper" in battle. Take a look, for instance, at Exodus 18:4, Deuteronomy 33:7, and Psalm 33:20 which reads, "We wait in hope for the Lord; he is our help and our shield."

God is subordinate to no one. The term indicates a supportive role of offering strength at the right times in the right ways.

A wife's number one priority is to support, affirm, and empower her husband to fulfill the calling God has given him inside and outside the home. This is critical, and it explains why a good wife is so highly valued in Scripture.

"An excellent wife, who can find? For her worth is far above jewels. The heart of her husband trusts in her, and he will have no lack of gain. She does him good and not evil all the days of her life" (Prov. 31:10–12 NASB).

The "heart of her husband" feeds off the support of his wife. One of a man's biggest secrets is his insecurity. He wonders how things are going to play out when the pressure is on. One of his greatest needs is for respect or honor. Deep down, he wonders, *Am I really a man? Do I have what it takes?* A wife's yes—in her actions and her words—gives him strength. And it causes his heart to trust her.

The wife is to be her husband's champion—a supportive teammate and best friend. Organizations that thrive always have champions, people who are zealous for the cause, who embrace the values, and who dedicate themselves to the mission. They are the glue that keeps the organization together. The wife is the most powerful influence in the family, and when she is committed to the cause and says, "We can do this," she becomes the glue that holds everything together. She champions the things that matter most.

Five Relational Objectives

There are many ways a wife can champion her husband in different seasons, but there are at least five objectives:

1. Make time with God your number one priority.

2. Pray for your husband regularly.

3. Plan for him daily.

4. Prepare for him daily.

5. Protect your time with him.

1. Make time with God your number one priority.

You have the most demanding job in the world, spiritually, emotionally, and physically. You are constantly multitasking as you are pulled at by multiple people to meet multiple needs in and out of the home. You understand that running a home is more than making sure people have food and clothes. You realize that it is a transformational organization where love is created, received, and exported. The home shapes the direction of human lives.

> *The only way you can run a home as a transformational, loving environment is with God's help.*

Psychologists talk a lot about the dynamics of our family of origin. Everyone lives with the experiences of their early lives, carrying the strengths and weaknesses of what their parents did or did not provide. That early environment shapes who we are. Women understand that, and it can feel like an overwhelming responsibility. The only way you can run a home as a transformational, loving environment is with God's help. You need strength and wisdom.

Time for yourself and to be connected from the heart with other women is important too; that creates space for getting into the Bible, developing mentoring relationships, and allowing others to speak Jesus's truth into your life. But time alone with him is essential.

My wife has understood this for as long as I can remember. Even when we were young and did not always know what we were doing as parents—and when we went to marriage counseling early in our marriage to sort out a lot of the issues we were having—this was one constant for her. She made meeting with God her top priority. Sometimes that was only five or ten minutes before a baby awakened or twenty minutes before the kids got up, but I would often find her talking with God and reading God's Word at 5:30 in the morning. She understood how important that was.

2. Pray for your husband regularly.

Susanna Wesley had nineteen children, only ten of whom survived past infancy. The family often lived at the edge of poverty, and her husband was jailed twice for financial issues. Life was difficult, and Susanna was her children's primary source of education, so her hands were full.

According to one story told about her, she would often go outside and sit on a stump, with children running and playing all around her, and pull her apron over her head to pray for each one of them and for her husband. She knew she needed God, his wisdom, and his power to be a wife, mother, and godly influence in her home. She could not impart what she didn't possess; she had to give to her family from what God had given her. She made sure she received from him regularly. Two of her sons, John and Charles, grew up to change the world in some powerful ways.

One of the greatest promises a praying wife has among her spiritual resources is Proverbs 21:1: "The king's heart is like a stream of water directed by the LORD; he guides it wherever he pleases" (NLT). This is not just about kings' hearts; it applies to men, women, and children everywhere.

I've seen my wife rely on this promise again and again. She would have an issue with me, talk about it, make suggestions, and encourage me to read a book on that topic with her, and my heart still would not change. Then she would go to God.

> *God longs to hear a wife and mother pray for her husband and children. He responds in very powerful ways.*

"Lord, Chip isn't listening to me. Please take this into your own hands. Get under his skin. Show him what he needs to know in order to lead this family well."

And very often—not always, because this isn't about manipulation, and on occasion I might have actually been right—God would begin to work in my heart and mind to change me. Theresa learned that the greatest ally in accomplishing an impossible task, especially those related to the hearts and minds of her husband and children, is prayer: to ask God, seek God, and knock on the doors of heaven. God longs to hear a wife and mother pray for her husband and children. He responds in very powerful ways.

3. Plan for your husband daily.

There are two ways to go through life: letting it happen to you, or being proactive and managing it. Most people do at least a little of both, but with all the demands placed on you in your family life, and with all the juggling you will do, you need to be intentional. Somewhere in that mix of juggling and planning, you need to be purposeful about caring for your husband.

Sometimes that may be a simple act of kindness—putting a special note somewhere for him to find or lighting candles for your dinner together. Maybe you find a way to get the kids out of the house for a little while so you can have some time to be alone together. Whatever you choose to do, it is important to plan for your husband, just as it is important for him to carve time out of his schedule for you.

> *You will find that whatever you invest in will grow, and whatever you neglect will eventually die.*

You will find that whatever you invest in will grow, and whatever you neglect will eventually die. That's true in almost any area of life, especially in your relationships. We don't necessarily get what we hope for; we tend to get what we plan for. Intending something to happen rarely makes it happen. We have to structure our days for desired outcomes. Structure results in outcomes.

That's what wives and moms have to do—for every person in the family. Find ways to invest in your husband with tangible signs of honor, respect, and love—even if he does not seem to respond at first. Eventually, he will clue in and he will love it. As you begin to meet some needs in his life, he will start to lead a little better and love a little deeper.

4. Prepare for your husband daily.

Women do a lot to attract a man in the early days of their relationship. As time goes on, those efforts can be smothered by responsibilities with children and work. I understand that, and it would be completely unrealistic to expect the relationship to continue forever just as it was when you were dating. But think back to those times when you got excited about seeing him. How did you prepare then? Did you open the door wearing baggy sweatpants and no makeup? Probably not. You prepared to present your best self to him.

Over time and under pressure, we spouses get so familiar with each other that the desire to leave our best impression fades away. That's normal—to a degree. None of us will look like a twenty-year-old on a date for the rest of our lives. It would be unrealistic to spend our lives at a gym, invest in the most fashionable wardrobe, look and smell our best every day of every decade, and always get excited about seeing each other.

But there is a big difference between adjusting to the years and giving in to them, and being casual and being apathetic. Desire can get quenched under the demands of daily life. Couples need to keep the physical, emotional, and relational sparks alive, and part of that is preparing for each other.

God created men to be visually attracted to women. A husband typically is out in the world seeing other women who have determined to look and smell their best for everyone else. He does not need to come home to a perfect wife, but he does need to see a spark in her from time to time that reminds him she's still interested, which reignites his own interest.

A wife who prepares for her husband visually, emotionally, and relationally can make a big difference in the way he thinks about her and interacts with her.

Despite limited salary and four children, we had a personal conviction for Theresa to be a full-time homemaker during our children's formative years. It was a big assignment, yet I remember her setting aside time to put on fresh makeup, and she looked great when I walked in the door. Forty years later, she still takes the time to prepare for me, and it really matters.

This can be very difficult with all the demands placed on each of your lives, especially if both of you have an income-earning job. You often feel obligated to meet other people's needs above each other's. I remember how often I would answer the phone when cell phones first became common-place. On one of my days off, Theresa once looked at me and said, "Do you want to be with me, or are you going to talk on the phone all the time?"

"Just taking a quick call," I assured her.

"You're always taking a quick call. I feel like taking that thing and throwing it away." (Those are my sweet wife's strong words.) I got the point. My attention was constantly being taken away from her. Many wives have a tendency to do the same thing—to fill the time with their husbands with quick conversations or mundane distractions. Be intentional about what occupies your attention. Plan to connect with your husband, and you'll be glad you did.

5. *Protect your time with your husband.*

Apart from your relationship with God, your marriage is the most important relationship you have. Your husband will feel empowered when he sees you saying no to the children or to other demands and interests that might make him feel like he's second place in your life. Don't neglect your other responsibilities, of course, but do always make him feel like he is your priority.

> *Apart from your relationship with God, your marriage is the most important relationship you have.*

You may feel that these five objectives are piling extra demands on you and stretching you beyond your capacity. In a sense, that's true; you will need supernatural help to be the woman God has called you to be. But in another sense, these objectives are less about adding responsibilities and more about removing *false* responsibilities so you can be the woman God designed you to be.

You do not need to take on extra burdens; you are being called to step into genuine, biblical femininity. You are fully equipped for that already, so be encouraged. You have everything you need—including the help of the Holy Spirit and plenty of grace as you grow—to do what you are called to do and, just as importantly, *not* do what you haven't been called to do.

Carve out the time to answer the following questions and look through the recommended resources below. Change doesn't happen unless something changes!

_____ Questions for Reflection and Discussion _____

1. What was most helpful in this chapter for you? Why?

2. Which of the five practices discussed in this chapter do you find come most naturally to you?

3. Which of the five practices do you sense needs some additional attention or focus from you? Why?

4. What's the biggest barrier or challenge you are facing in nurturing your husband? Your family?

5. Who could help you take those next steps to nurture and love your husband the way you want and need to?

Recommended Resources

The Read Scripture app, available on Google Play and the App Store (an amazing resource to help develop consistent routines of connecting with God through his Word)

The Power of a Praying Wife, by Stormie Omartian

Sermon audio: "Communication—How to Share Hearts Instead of Exchange Words" (livingontheedge.org/marriagethatworksresources)

Sermon audio and affirmation cards: "Precious in His Sight," by Theresa Ingram (livingontheedge.org/marriagethatworksresources)

12

Stepping In as a Woman: *Protect*

Your second priority as a woman is to create an environment in the home that nurtures and develops your children to fulfill God's will for their lives but also minimizes harmful influences. You are a shaper and protector of young hearts. The most influential people in the world are mothers. Period.

Great men of God like John and Charles Wesley first saw faith in their mothers, who gave them acceptance, confidence, an understanding of themselves and the world, and examples of devotion. When the camera turns to a football player who just made a great play, what does he say? "Hi, Mom!" Studies show that in every area other than moral development and sexual identity, in which fathers play a critical role, moms are by far the most powerful influence in their children's lives. Your priority as protector is vital not only to your family but also to the world your children will live in.

Scripture gives many examples of spiritual protection in the home, but one of the clearest statements is given in the context of young women in early church times whose husbands had died.

In the culture of the times, a young widow essentially had two options other than remarriage: to dedicate herself to the church and let the church support her financially or to become a prostitute. It was difficult for women to earn a living or live independently in Bible times. There were exceptions: women like Lydia in Acts 16 and some of the women who supported Jesus financially (Luke 8:1–3) were unusually self-sufficient. But often, single women were in a precarious position. So Paul wrote, "I counsel younger widows to marry, to have children, to manage their homes and to give the enemy no opportunity for slander" (1 Tim. 5:14).

The literal meaning of the words in this sentence imply that a married woman is to make things happen in the home—to be the chief operating officer, the COO, of her household. She sets direction and develops systems that enable her family to grow in love and have their needs met.

Somehow society has convinced many women that if motherhood is the only job they ever have, they are wasting their lives. This amazing, esteemed, God-given assignment has been dismissed as peripheral or unimportant to real life, and real fulfillment must therefore lie in accomplishing something else. Scripture says the opposite is true. Mothers have a unique opportunity to shape lives and empower the next generation to follow God faithfully. A mother is the key teacher, counselor, consoler, and refuge for her children, and her impact in their lives is unequaled.

Like the actress whose story opened chapter 10, many female celebrities have recently rediscovered their desire to be mothers. Many of them are single—it seems to be a trend in Hollywood now for unmarried women to adopt or get pregnant outside of a committed relationship—but it is happening more and more, especially to those who reach their forties and realize they have been missing something they were made to do. Even women who have had children earlier are adopting in greater numbers, as if they have suddenly realized that being a mother matters.

I realize not every woman will become a mother, and some who desperately want to bear a child may never get to have that experience. But those who do invest their lives in motherhood need to understand that even in a culture that marginalizes that identity, it is a high and holy calling.

Five Spiritual Objectives

Your priority as protector of your family involves these five objectives:

1. Model dependency on Christ.

2. Pray for your children fervently.

3. Create structures and scheduled times that make family life a priority.

4. Teach your children how to live.

5. Make time for your children.

1. Model dependency on Christ.

Contrary to what most parents believe, your children will not end up doing what you have told them. They will end up being like you. Your example matters much more than your words; behavior is generally caught, not taught. Jesus expressed the same principle: "Everyone who is fully trained will be like their teacher" (Luke 6:40).

How you think, how you drive, what you say when you're stressed, how you respond in a crisis, the ways you love God, the manner in which you treat your husband—all of these attitudes and behaviors are being passed on to your children. They will choose to modify some of those responses as they get older, of course. Most kids decide to do some things differently than their parents. But to do so, they will have to depart from what came to them naturally—your example. So the greatest gift you can give yourself as wife to your husband and mother to your children is a lifestyle that is dependent on Jesus.

One of my sons went through a season of rebellion that was really painful for us and for him as well. He has since become a godly husband, father, and prolific writer of Christian music, but it took a while. Shortly after that season ended, I asked him what made the difference for him. What was it that caused him to turn so powerfully back to his relationship with Christ? It wasn't one of my persuasive sermons but something even more gratifying.

"Dad," he said, "Jesus is so real to Mom and you, and your lives are so authentic. And when I rebelled, I didn't see you get uptight about what people at church would think. I saw tears come down your faces because I didn't embrace the Jesus that you love."

> *When you model dependency on Jesus, you are painting a picture day by day of what truly matters.*

What was he really saying? That children emulate what really matters to us. When you model dependency on Jesus, you are painting a picture day by day of what truly matters.

2. Pray for your children fervently.

If you're a mother, you know by now how little control you have over your children's choices, especially as they get older. When they eventually leave home, their decisions, values, and priorities are beyond your direct influence. The sense of control we have as parents is generally an illusion anyway, but that becomes painfully apparent as time goes on. You do the best you can and teach them what you know, but they will still have to make decisions in the heat of the moment, respond to peer pressure, and choose their own values.

You will not be there to enforce your will. So you talk to your heavenly Father a lot—specifically and earnestly. One of the most powerful things you can do for your kids is to pray for them fervently.

Make sure your prayers cover more than just the externals of their lives—like good grades, good health, and good friends. Pray that they would hunger and thirst for righteousness, that they would seek God with all their heart, that they would have a passion for God's holiness. Ask God to give them wisdom in choosing friends and the strength to resist temptation. Expect him to work in your children's lives.

Let me offer a word of caution here, however. Don't judge your prayers by how quickly God answers them. At times, he will dramatically intervene, but not always. Instead, see your prayers as seeds being planted in your children's lives that will one day bear fruit or as small investments that will grow over time into abundant returns. Sometimes the results of a mother's prayers are not seen until the child is grown. But be persistent, and don't give up. Your prayers *are* being answered, and you *are* making a difference.

3. Create structures and scheduled times that make family life a priority.

You are the COO of the home, and there will be times when you have to lay down the law. You will have to decide what structure or schedule you are going to have for mealtimes, bedtimes, days off, vacations, and any other time when family life needs to take priority over other activities. You may have to enforce dinnertime, at least on certain nights of the week, as a time when all phones and devices are off, no ball games are playing in the background, and everyone is together. Speed kills relationships—and if everyone is always running around doing their own thing, relationships will weaken and break down.

The mother is the glue that keeps binding those relationships. But if you only hope for family time, it won't happen. You have to schedule it. Structures, not intentions, result in outcomes.

4. Teach your children how to live.

I believe that the most powerful teacher in any person's life is his or her mother. You will have the deepest connection with your children. You have known your children longer than anyone else, by at least nine months. And for the first few months after birth, you are your child's dominant caretaker. The bonding that occurs during pregnancy and the early months of infancy has more impact on a child's early life than any other influence. That bond creates an extremely powerful connection and trust for teaching your children how to live.

Almost all mothers know how to train their children in behavioral issues—using good manners, making polite conversation, treating other people well, and that sort of thing. And most do not need suggestions for other things to try. But if you're looking for ideas beyond the basics, here are a few I've observed over the years:

- *Teach your children to read, even before they begin school.*

  Theresa did this with our children, and they learned to love reading early. That is an extremely valuable and influential activity that increases their intellectual capacity and academic opportunities.

- *Teach them to pray.*

  Even when they are small, they can have meaningful conversations with God.

- *Teach them—girls and boys—to cook.*

  Boys (and girls) need to know how to take care of themselves.

- *Teach them to listen well.*

  Noticing what other people are feeling and thinking is a skill everyone needs.

- *Teach them to celebrate.*

  We live in a fast-paced world that is so focused on performance that many people don't know how to stop and enjoy the journey.

- *Teach them to be generous.*

  After all, our God is infinitely generous.

- *Teach them a craft, a musical instrument, a sport, or a skill that requires using their hands.*

  This develops not only their motor skills and discipline, it helps strengthen their creativity and imagination.

- *Teach them how to speak in public.*

  Verbal communication is a declining skill, and people who have it will have an advantage socially and in many career fields.

- *Teach them to resolve conflict.*

  Avoiding conflict leads to problems. Learning to dispassionately address issues with people will be an extremely useful skill throughout their professional and personal life.

- *Teach them how to relax and not feel guilty.*

  After all, the Lord rested on the Sabbath!

You won't cover all the possibilities, and none of them will happen overnight. But work some of these into your children's lives, even if it's just for ten or fifteen minutes a day in certain seasons. Your kids will learn some valuable skills that will serve them well the rest of their lives.

You and your husband are ultimately responsible—not as controllers, but as the main influencers—for how your kids think, relate, and value God and others. The school, the church, and other caretakers may play a role, but they are not primary. You are. You will give them the direction they need to learn and grow spiritually, emotionally, intellectually, relationally, and physically. Take the initiative and be intentional about teaching them what they need to know in life.

5. Make time for your children.

Be available. The best things in life rarely happen on your official schedule. The teachable moments and the memorable conversations come up between the items on the to-do list, so you have to leave some time between those tasks.

That isn't easy; you already juggle a lot of demands on your time. But think about what really matters. What is going on in your children's hearts? When is your daughter going to open up and talk about the huge fear she is facing or the relationship that is playing with her emotions? When is your son going to open up about the struggles he deals with or the insecurities that are eating at him? You can't schedule those conversations—they just happen—but you can create space for them. (Warning: this almost always involves setting some very strong limits on TV, phones, video games, and computer activities.)

> *Create a world in which you are not always going somewhere, accomplishing something, or listening to something.*

If you have developed a good relationship with your children and have quiet moments when they can open up, you may be amazed at what comes out of them sometimes. And you will be grateful that you were available to walk them through their challenges and concerns.

Don't let the typical North American lifestyle of being stressed, overworked, and overwhelmed deprive you of valuable moments with your children that you and they will never forget. Create a world in which you are not always going somewhere, accomplishing something, or listening to something. Boredom is the birthplace of spontaneity and creativity, and it's one of the most underappreciated gifts you can give your children. Make time just to hang out, and some pretty exciting things might happen.

Mentoring Younger Wives

Another area of a wife's protective priority mentioned in Scripture is toward younger women. The Bible says to train younger women in the art of becoming godly wives and mothers. In other words, if you have learned the art of family relationships, you need to pass that knowledge down to future generations. If you are learning that art now, you need to glean wisdom from those who have gone before you. This is one of the ways God has arranged for protecting and preserving a biblical culture among his people.

In the book of Titus, Paul is writing to the pastor of a church on the island of Crete, where women were known for being a little wilder than elsewhere, somewhat like today's celebrity bad girls. Paul even refers to the island's reputation for immorality and a lack of ethics.

In Titus 2:3–5, he instructs Christian women to impart something of their reverence and devotion to younger women who are still learning what God's Word teaches about family relationships. Why? So that the Word of God will not be dishonored.

> Likewise, teach the older women to be reverent in the way they live, not to be slanderers or addicted to much wine, but to teach what is good. Then they can urge the younger women to love their husbands and children, to be self-controlled and pure, to be busy at home, to be kind, and to be subject to their husbands, so that no one will malign the word of God.

In other words, people need to see homes where lives are transformed, where love, acceptance, affirmation, and intimacy in marriage are practiced and celebrated. Homes that do not function that way call into question what we believe. Homes that do function that way become a testimony of the transforming power of God's Word.

We used to live in a world where grandmothers and extended families lived close to each other and each generation would pass down its wisdom to the next. Husbands and wives learned how to resolve conflict and raise children from their parents and grandparents. Not many people experience that dynamic anymore. Many of us have families who live on the other side of the country or even on other continents.

It's left to a young woman to sort out the right box top from all the other options the culture gives her. She is taught to be well educated, to be pretty, to find the right man, to have a great career, to make a lot of money, and to be upwardly mobile, and then to consider whether or not she ought to have kids. And if she does, should she stay home with them or send them to a daycare or create some hybrid options to fit her unique needs? How should she raise them in today's world? She needs the advice of an older, godly woman to sort out all her options and navigate her challenges, and she may not find one in her extended family.

Some more mature women may not be convinced they have anything to offer. I've heard the humility: "Oh, I just raised three kids. By God's grace, they turned out better than we deserve. We may not have the most exciting marriage, but we've somehow managed to keep it together and love each other deeply for forty years. I guess it works."

If that sounds like you, there is more wisdom in those forty years than you realize. With a little bit of encouragement and training, you could actually be one of the greatest difference makers in the lives of younger wives. And if you are a young wife, find a more experienced one who is willing to mentor you. Times may have changed, but human nature and family dynamics are a lot like they always have been. You may have a wider range of choices than many women of the past, but a lot of women who have made some of those choices can tell you how fulfilling (or not) some of them are.

The church is full of women of every age who have found success as our culture defines it and are now trying to figure out how to be really fulfilled, and they need cross-generational relationships. They need to know how God's plan has worked in the lives of women who have lived it. They need someone to talk through the important questions of work and children and marriage with them. There is no "one size fits all." Different women have different gifts and challenges. God will show you how to navigate your specific situation as you commit to fully follow his design.

> *Don't be overwhelmed by the role God has given you as a wife.*

So don't be overwhelmed by the role God has given you as a wife. It is extremely significant, but it is also a perfect match for the gifts he has placed within you. If no one recognizes that you are shaping history by influencing your husband and children—God sees. You may have a more prominent role outside your home at certain stages of life, but even when you feel like you aren't doing anything significant, you can rest assured that you are. You are a vital part of God's plan, and he will empower you in every way you serve those around you. Even more, you will eventually see the fruit of your labor in the lives of those you love.

Answer the following questions and then pray about steps you can take to strengthen areas of your life as a wife and mother. Consider using the listed resources too.

Questions for Reflection and Discussion

1. What was most helpful in this chapter for you? Why?

2. Which of the five practices discussed in this chapter do you find come most naturally to you?

3. Which of the five practices do you sense needs some additional attention or focus from you? Why?

4. What's the biggest barrier or challenge you are facing in protecting your husband? Your family?

5. Who could help you take those next steps to protect your husband and family the way you want and need to?

Recommended Resources

The Power of a Praying Mom, by Stormie Omartian

Sermon series: "Precious in His Sight," by Theresa Ingram (this series covers what Theresa taught our daughter about her identity and self-image) (livingontheedge.org/marriagethatworksresources)

Sermon audio: "How to Fight Fair in Marriage" (conflict resolution is critical in marriage and family; this message will teach you how to attack the issues rather than the person) (livingontheedge.org/marriagethat worksresources)

13

Stepping In as a Woman: *Provide*

You will find that you provide for your husband and children in a variety of ways, many of them having little to do with finances. You may be much more hands-on in managing the budget than your husband is, but as the one who often takes care of the necessities and details of daily life, your provision also includes matters of diet, health, clothing, instruction, and much more. The financial aspect of your role is not your highest priority.

But one of the questions that always comes up in discussing a woman's role in the home is her potential role outside of it. Should she have an income-earning job? And the short answer I always give to that question is, "It depends."

That question should be asked only after other priorities are well established and covered. If your marriage is your highest priority and you are fulfilling your responsibilities as a champion for your husband and a mother for your children, if you have them, then it is reasonable to consider whether, when, how, and why you should work outside the home.

Many factors come into play: the ages and stages of your kids, your energy level, your personality and gifts, and your capacity. But it is always important to remember what research tells us about how children develop and mature.

For the first six to eight years of a child's life, his or her personality will be formed through the parent-child bond, and specifically through the mother-child bond. Children's personalities are like wet cement at that age. They are forming their values, morals, sense of security, and understanding of what life is all about. Whatever it takes, you want to be around for that.

So how much is a second job, a second car, or a nice home worth? That's a really important question to ask before you take on a mortgage payment, get that extra job to pay for it, and put your hopes in the character of the person spending those precious hours each day with your child.

I taught this a number of years ago, and a young Christian came up to me afterward to ask if we could talk. He had been a believer for only a few years, so he had not built up all the justifications and excuses a lot of us come up with to sound spiritual and still do what we want.

"I have a decent job and my wife is a teacher. With both of our incomes, we can afford to live in Santa Cruz," he said. At the time, our area of California was the second-most expensive place to live in the US. "But we can't live here on one income. We believe after hearing your talk about God's design for the family that we need to move so she can stay at home with our two kids."

"That's a big step for you all; are you sure?" I asked.

"Yeah. We really enjoy living here, but if we stay, twenty years from now we will wish we had spent our time, energy, and money on the things that matter most. We're moving to Oregon."

All I could tell him was, "I'll miss you all, but I think you are making a wise decision."

Three years later, I got a letter from him. "Chip, it's the greatest decision we ever made," he wrote. "Maybe we can move back one day when our kids get older, but for now, this was the right thing to do. Our marriage and family are thriving."

It's great to live where you want to live and have the kind of cars and home you want to have, but these are not priorities. God may move you somewhere else so you can reprioritize your family life. There is no law that says you have to own a home, build up equity, or work outside the house to achieve some kind of financial security. I don't mean to sound negative, but during thirty-five years pastoring and counseling God's people, I've watched countless couples end up with a nice house and plenty of money but with kids who don't know them very well, don't walk with God, and don't spend time with their parents. It's tragic. Sometimes the right choices are the hardest ones.

> *Sometimes the right choices are the hardest ones.*

191

God will honor the right choices. I know that from experience, and I also know how hard those choices can be.

Our third child came along when I was going to seminary full-time and working a full-time job. I made $1,000 a month, but Theresa and I were committed to her being home to nurture and protect our children. So I got up at 4 a.m. every day, did my schoolwork, and went to classes until dinner. Then I ate dinner, spent some time with the family, and went to work until 11 p.m. or midnight. I slept four or five hours on weeknights and then made up for it a little on weekends. We lived in government-subsidized housing and had one car without air-conditioning—in Texas. We would go to a doughnut shop for our dates because they gave free refills on coffee. We'd buy one doughnut and split it. It was an incredibly difficult time of life. God provided at just the right times, like someone giving us a bag of groceries or an unexpected check coming in the mail. Our kids lived on peanut butter and honey sandwiches with bread Theresa made from scratch almost every day for nearly five years.

At one point when we were having trouble paying our bills, we had a neighbor with a five-year-old and an infant who had been abandoned by her husband. We felt led to pay her rent for her, and it was kind of terrifying—we paid the $236 in government-subsidized housing, but it left us with only about $15 in our checking account, and our rent was going to be due in a couple weeks.

The due date came, and we just didn't have any money. I felt stupid. Of course, Theresa was convinced God would provide. We had a three-day grace period to submit our rent check, and on day one I was pointing out Philippians 4:19 to God with more than a hint of accusation in my attitude, reminding him that he was supposed to provide. But nothing came.

Then on the third day, I got a letter with a football insignia on it and a Lombardi Avenue return address. It had come from the home of the Green Bay Packers.

It was from a guy I had met seven or eight years earlier, when he played basketball for one of my friends who was a coach. He later went to college in California to play quarterback and was eventually drafted and played professional ball. All these years later, he contacted my friend the coach and said, "Remember that guy who led the Bible study back when you were coaching me? I can't get him off my mind. I think I'm supposed to send him some money. Do you know how I could get in touch with him?"

So out of the blue, an NFL quarterback was praying, without having any idea about our needs, and he sent a check for $1,000 that arrived at exactly the right time to pay our rent. I could tell at least another dozen stories like that.

I'm not saying it's wrong for moms to work; we make different decisions at different times, depending on our situations and changing priorities. But for us, it was a step of faith and obedience for Theresa to stay home with the kids, and even though that was a hard time, I don't even see it as a sacrifice today. We decided we would rather be poor in finances and rich in family relationships. It was a short season and I wouldn't trade it for anything.

I realize many families would make different decisions in those circumstances. All I can tell you is that your role as a champion, a mother, and a mentor will pay more dividends than the extra money you can bring in during your children's critical early years.

> One study suggested that the average couple's income increases by only about 15 percent when they both work.

Sometimes that extra money doesn't amount to very much additional income after you account for all the issues that come with a second job—the work wardrobe, gas in the second car, childcare expenses, taxes, and the amount of time and money you spend eating out because neither spouse has time to cook. One study suggested that the average couple's income increases by only about 15 percent when they both work.

Again, I'm not saying it's wrong for a woman to work. Proverbs 31 commends a wife for being industrious and earning income. But there are a lot of things to consider, especially when your children are young.

Supporting Single Mothers

The question that always comes up at this point is, What about single mothers? Sometimes a woman has very little choice about whether to earn an income or not. I wish I had an easy answer and unlimited financial resources to help single parents. It is one of the most demanding and difficult assignments for a parent. I believe the church can play a vital role in relational and even financial support in times of crisis, and I have watched God sustain single moms who have to work to support their families. I believe the grace of God is sufficient to cover your children and care for your needs, but the cost is high and we, the body of Christ, need to support each other to make up for what you cannot do on your own.

Working single moms tend to feel guilty and exhausted. God does not require of you what you cannot accomplish. If you do not have a husband around, you are carrying more weight than most women have to carry. Seek out a Bible-teaching church to be a part of your kids' lives and don't be ashamed to ask for help. Ask God for the miraculous provision of friendship, role models for your children, and finances in times of need.

That's good advice in any situation. Life is full of challenges and hard decisions, and the bottom line is you'll have to ask the Holy Spirit for guidance and follow him as he directs your steps. As uncertain as that can feel sometimes, you can be confident that God has a lot of grace for those who seek him. His own promises keep him zealously seeking your welfare. He is committed to taking care of you; you can rest confidently in him.

Finally, as you read the paragraphs above, who is a single mom that could really use your help, support, friendship, and financial support? If we really care about women, this is an opportunity for us to practice what we believe. God's grace usually comes through ordinary people like you and me who decide to proactively help those in need.

Husbands Need to Help

Finally, just as wives help their husbands fulfill their priorities, husbands need to help their wives fulfill theirs. Your job, men, is helping your wife be the best COO she can be.

In most homes, women do the lion's share of the organizational and maintenance tasks—washing, cleaning, shopping, cooking, balancing the checkbook, waking the kids up and getting them dressed, and so on. I recommend that the husband list all the jobs that need to happen for the home to function and identify who currently owns each responsibility, then figure out some significant ways to lighten his wife's load.

Refuse to let your wife bear all the burden. I'm not much of a cook, unlike all my sons and daughter, but I do the dishes, vacuum, and share the errands, and I have honestly learned to enjoy doing it. It's our responsibility as men to make sure our wives have some time to spend with other women. I met a man recently who brought his daughters to the gym with their coloring books so his wife could go to a Bible study with her friends. Be creative. Find ways to create some margin in her life. With your actions, tell her that you are in this with her and want to help her out.

That attitude makes a great picture of mutual submission, which takes us back to where we started. It is the foundation of all relationships in the home, and it feeds the marriage relationship in ways that allow each person to grow individually and in deeper intimacy with each other. It cultivates the kind of intimacy we see in the Trinity, where the Father, Son, and Spirit overflow with divine love one for another. A good marriage is a beautiful dance that reflects the nature of God, is deeply fulfilling to each partner, and is a blessing to everyone who sees it.

_____ **Questions for Reflection and Discussion** _____

1. Why does a man need a champion on his side? In what ways can a wife fulfill this role to nurture her husband?

2. Why are mothers so important in the lives of their children? What do they provide for their children that no other person can provide?

3. Why do you think Scripture singles out the mentoring role for women in matters of marriage and family? In what ways do you think this is needed in modern times?

4. If you are a woman, which of your three roles—nurturer, protector, or provider—do you find to be most challenging? What do you need to do to overcome those challenges?

5. In what ways has this chapter helped you understand the process of creating the family dynamics you want to experience? What specific steps can you take now to move toward your family goals?

14

How to Make It through the Hard Times

We've seen a lot of natural disasters over the last few years—devastating hurricanes and flooding in places like New Orleans, Houston, and the Caribbean; mudslides and fires in California; earthquakes and violent storms in many regions of the world. In some cases, these events do not come with any warnings. But when they do, we can be sure of one thing: those who are prepared and responsive to the warnings have a much better chance of surviving than those who are not.

As we come near to the end of this journey, I think it's important to warn you about the possibility of storms coming your way. If you are unprepared, these storms could devastate your marriage. But if you are prepared and know how to respond, you can come through them unscathed—even stronger. It all depends on your expectations, your understanding of the situation, and your willingness to make preparations.

Some storms in marriage are very predictable. In this chapter, I want to share some of them with you. I didn't see them coming in my marriage, and Theresa and I experienced a lot of difficult challenges and stress as a result. After more than four decades of my own experiences as a husband, pastor, and counselor of married couples, I can now look back and see how a little bit of preparation would have helped us— and how an underlying belief and commitment that many couples have not yet grasped can make *all* the difference.

Weathering the Storms

Not every storm in marriage will fit into a specific category, but there are some predictable kinds of challenges we all face. Some of the most common ones look like this.

Storm #1: "I Can't Believe They Did That"

When you first get married, the euphoria and the infatuation can run pretty high for a while. We call this the honeymoon period. It's a wonderful season of marriage and a beautiful part of God's design. But eventually that first fight comes. I remember the first major fight Theresa and I had, and it was over something that, looking back now, seems ridiculous. But what we fought about wasn't nearly as disturbing to me as the fact that someone I loved so much could make me feel so angry and disillusioned—and only a few weeks into our life together as husband and wife.

I didn't know how to resolve anger at the time. I was caught completely off guard. I found myself slamming the door, getting in my car, driving around for two hours, and actually telling God that I may have made the biggest mistake of my life. I can look back on it and laugh now, but I certainly wasn't laughing then. And if you don't recognize the wounds that can come from an experience like that and view them as somewhat normal, you end up sowing seeds of distrust and resentment in your heart and your marriage.

> *Whatever it takes, find a safe place to share your frustrations, both individually and as a couple.*

I have always believed in the importance of premarital counseling, but I have also found that postmarital counseling in the first few months of marriage can be vital. Sometimes that may come from a professional counselor or a pastor, but even getting advice from an older couple can help you prepare for and weather the early storms. Just taking that step will help you learn some basic communication skills, begin to understand how your mate works, and recognize that what you are going through is normal. Whatever it takes, find a safe place to share your frustrations, both individually and as a couple.

Storm #2: The New Baby

One of the greatest joys you can ever have is bringing a new life into the world with the person you love. But that great joy can also be the occasion for one of the greatest storms in your marriage. Pregnancy is not an easy time for many couples. The wife doesn't always feel good and may not be very affectionate, and the husband may be surprised at how the dynamics of the relationship change during pregnancy and shortly after the baby's birth. Men tend not to understand how vulnerable their wives feel and do not realize that they will need to be far more sensitive than ever before. And women tend to assume that their husbands will naturally understand fatigue, mood swings, and negative remarks and attitudes. Many of these tendencies and assumptions are not verbalized; communication becomes absolutely critical.

Sexual intimacy can be a sensitive subject in this season of marriage. It is possible nearly throughout the entire pregnancy, but it is often a casualty of the process, and the impact on the man is usually more traumatic than it is on the woman. She is dealing with all kinds of emotions and changes in her body, and the way she deals with them can feel to the man like subtle forms of rejection. That is not her intent, of course—far from it. But he is not getting the physical and emotional validation he craves, and even though he knows he needs to be more sensitive to her needs than ever before, the lack of intimacy begins to do strange work in his brain and emotions. Some men find that their greatest times of temptation are during the season of their wife's pregnancy. Just knowing that ahead of time can be helpful in weathering that storm.

The storm doesn't end as soon as the baby is born. I will never forget the joy and excitement of the first few weeks after our first child together was born. We were euphoric parents with this wonderful bundle of a miracle God had given us. But after about six weeks of being as patient and sensitive as I knew how to be, I began to notice the fact that my wife's full attention, all her emotions and affection, were on a seven-pound bundle of joy and not on me. Intellectually, I understood why. But by the third month, I was developing quite a bit of resentment. She didn't want to go out. She couldn't leave the baby even for an hour to go get a cup of coffee. Even after six months, Theresa still didn't trust anyone to take care of our child without one of us being there. We never had any time alone.

One of the worst feelings I can remember was being jealous of a little baby whom I loved with all my heart. This miraculous event was changing our relationship in some really difficult ways. It isn't easy for a man to tell his wife that he is jealous of their child. It seems selfish and insensitive. But as important as this season is, marriage always takes priority. A woman will find it very stretching to recognize that as wonderful as this new baby is, she still needs to direct some of her emotional energy to her husband. He needs to see and feel that the marriage is still top priority. It wasn't easy for Theresa to take the big step of getting away from time to time, but eventually she did, and we made it through this wonderful but challenging time of our lives.

Storm #3: Growing Families and Workloads

Families tend to grow in the same seasons that careers get more demanding. All the diapers and demands of the preschool years added to the financial strain of a new family can stress you out. Older people will tell you again and again that it doesn't last forever, but it feels like it does. Husbands and wives will find themselves stretched in ways they have never been stretched before, and attitudes—toward each other and life in general—can deteriorate quickly.

A wife needs more help during this time than ever before and in many cases will have a young husband who doesn't quite understand everything she is going through. I often came home to a thoroughly exhausted wife, and I wasn't nearly as sensitive as I needed to be. I tried to be patient, but I felt the stresses too—demands at home and at work, with a domestic life I had never experienced and a career that was beginning to ramp up. For many couples, the overwhelming challenges of everyone in your life needing more energy and attention than you can give them creates a perfect storm that may cause a lot of relational friction and a tendency to drift apart. When marriage and family seem to be more of a sacrifice than a joy, endurance is critical.

> *When marriage and family seem to be more of a sacrifice than a joy, endurance is critical.*

Getting through this time was not easy for us. We had to learn some different communication skills. We found ways to get some breaks—time together and alone. We didn't have extended family nearby, but we shared our kids with other couples for time away, rearranged how we would get everything done at home and at work, and learned to partner together. We also believed what we had been told—that this time would not last forever—and kept going back to the commitment we had made to each other. It took everything we had. If you aren't prepared for storms, they can cause you to question your commitments. But the commitments last longer. Storms do pass.

Storm #4: The Teen Years

When your children hit the teen years, they are going through some pretty stressful challenges and changes of their own, which in turn creates stressful challenges and changes for you as a couple. The teen years are particularly taxing not only because your children are learning to spread their wings but also because their schedules can pull a family in fifty directions. The wife balances being counselor, chauffeur, cook, friend, and her husband's lover, often while trying to hold down full-time or part-time work. The husband is often at the prime of his career, with even greater demands being placed on him at work. Life can feel like it is nothing more than a never-ending act of spinning plates or putting out fires. Cultivating the marriage relationship is easily pushed to the margins or even completely out of the picture.

The most significant thing you can do in this season of life is to remind yourself of what is really important and consider whose voices and values you are going to listen to. As important as your family's work, school, and extracurricular activities may be, putting your marriage relationship first and foremost is the greatest influence you can have on your children. Eating together; blocking off time for you and your spouse to date; determining when, where, and how you are going to discipline the children; and keeping communication open on all issues will help you get through this storm. It may not be easy, and sometimes you may feel like you aren't succeeding. But if you keep your focus on your values and priorities, you will get through.

I don't believe the teenage years have to be as traumatic as people make them out to be. In many ways, they can be very exciting and fulfilling times. Some children navigate those years without much stress; others seem to create crises in their own lives and in your relationship with each other. We had a range of those experiences. But when you and your mate have different approaches to those experiences, the storm gets a bit more intense.

For whatever reason, people often marry someone who has the opposite view of how to discipline children. You may find that in the balance between truth and mercy, one of you leans toward truth and the other toward mercy. That tension can lead to incredible conflict. Our differences over disciplining our kids and keeping commitments resulted in a lot of late-night talks as we sat in bed to figure out what we were going to do and why, knowing we had to present a united front to our children. It takes a lot of time to get on the same page, but the process can make you stronger and keep you balanced as a person. The conflict isn't fun, but it can be very productive.

Just remember that counseling isn't only for people in trouble. Sometimes the best thing you can do is get outside help at the earliest sign of friction, whether that is formally through a counselor or pastor or informally by asking an older, wiser couple for advice.

Theresa and I found ourselves gravitating toward people who were ten or fifteen years older than we were and who had raised their kids well. Just gleaning some wisdom and insight from them was very helpful, and it reminded us that what we were going through was normal. Knowing that we were vulnerable in our relationship, we also found ourselves reading a lot of books on marriage, scheduling one or two weekends away each year, and making our weekly dates a priority. By "dates," I don't necessarily mean the romantic, "isn't life wonderful" kinds of experiences—though they are great if you have them. I mean we planned times to go out, be alone, and not talk about work or the kids and just have some fun.

Maintaining the relationship beyond work and parenting issues helps create trust and unity for dealing with those issues and having difficult conversations when you need to. Your marriage becomes the context for everything else rather than everything else taking priority over your marriage.

Storm #5: The Empty Nest

You may have noticed that most of the storms we have discussed so far come with a major change in your marriage or family, whether that change is an event or a new age and stage. Major changes shift the dynamics, and shifting dynamics create uncertainty and stress. That is true whether the change is adding a new child to the family, beginning a new job, moving to another place, or any other significant transition you face. You can navigate change when you have an unswerving commitment to— and good tools for—resolving conflict. Whether some of these transitions qualify as storms or just windows of vulnerability in the relationship may vary from couple to couple, but any of them can present a challenge.

> You can navigate change when you have an unswerving commitment to— and good tools for—resolving conflict.

One of those vulnerable times is the empty-nest season. After working so hard at our marriage, I assumed this would not be a tough time for us. We would have more time together, and it would be an exciting new experience. I could not have been more wrong. I greatly underestimated what it's like when a woman's God-given nurturing role goes through a radical shift. When kids leave the home, and especially if they are doing well, husbands often feel like it's a sign of a job well done and that a season of reward is beginning. For a wife, this can be a period of grief and loss.

We had some really challenging times, and I developed some resentment when Theresa was still feeling blue a few months after our last child left home. We went through that a little bit every time we dropped one of our children off at college, but when the last one left, it was one of the most difficult experiences I have seen my wife go through. It's one thing to understand that; it's another to live through it. As in the early stages of marriage and parenting, men have to develop an extra level of sensitivity.

That isn't easy, as we men are often going through changes during this time too. A man's energy and desires tend to diminish rapidly in midlife. Sometimes he begins to question whether he still "has it," if he's still attractive, if he can still be the man he longs to be. When those questions are paired with a woman's empty-nest vulnerability, the temptations can skyrocket. In the first five years, 20 percent of marriages end in divorce. On the other end, the divorce rate among adults ages 50 and older doubled between 1990 and 2010. Roughly 1 in 4 divorces in 2010 occurred to persons ages 50 and older, the typical period of empty-nesting.[1] You have to be prepared for that storm.

Obstacles Become Building Blocks

There are plenty of other marital storms. Infertility or miscarriages, trouble with in-laws, work disappointments, serious illnesses, or the death of a child. But I think the preceding five storms are predictable and touch almost every marriage. And preparation is the key to weathering them. If you know what is happening, prepare yourself, and have an unswerving commitment to each other, you'll be fine. In fact, you'll be more than fine; you'll come through the storms stronger and wiser. Instead of tearing you apart, the conflicts, difficulties, and differences will bond your hearts and minds together and build the kind of relationship that lasts.

The things that looked like obstacles to the kind of marriage you always dreamed of actually become the building blocks for that kind of marriage. The storms actually serve as catalysts to achieving your ultimate goal in marriage—oneness. But don't underestimate the cost, the struggle, or the temptations that will come with those storms.

If you are going through a hard time in your marriage, you may find it hard to believe that it will work out for your good, or even that you will be able to endure it. But it really is possible to have a marriage that is fulfilling spiritually, emotionally, and physically, even in the most trying times. The key is your and your spouse's comprehension of the very definition of marriage, which we'll discuss next.

Questions for Reflection and Discussion

1. What are a few of the characteristics of a "storm" in marriage? Do any of these hard times resonate with you? Why?

2. As I mentioned in this chapter, Theresa and I found ourselves gravitating toward people who were ten to fifteen years older than we were and who had raised their kids well. Who are the people in your life you can glean wisdom and insight from? Ask to meet up with them over coffee. What questions would you want to ask them?

3. Is there a couple you know going through a hard time in their marriage? How can you come alongside and help them through it?

4. What "predictable" storm could be coming your way, and what preparations can you make to help your marriage come out stronger in the end?

5. In the business of life, how are you making your marriage relationship a priority? Make a list of date ideas that give you time to be alone, talk, and have fun together.

15

Marriage: *Contract or Covenant?*

I f you were to ask your coworkers or friends, you might find couples who, if they're honest, wish they could trade in their spouse for a new model. Yet God has given us the means to rekindle the fires and keep them burning for life. But it involves letting go of our perceptions and embracing his definition of what a marriage really is. At a fundamental level, we have to understand the nature of marriage, what it is based on, and how God sees it. If we're missing that, we will not have the wisdom or endurance to follow the design to the end.

From outward appearances and many people's experiences, it often looks like the costs of marriage outweigh the benefits. Many people give up before they get to the payoff. From God's perspective—and ours, if we will trust him and align ourselves with his truth—the benefits far outweigh the costs, and we will enjoy those benefits if we embrace the true nature of the marriage covenant.

This issue of perspective is the reason some people lose their way in the storms and others come through them stronger. It all depends on their view of marriage. I believe one of the greatest determiners of marital fulfillment—and one of the greatest predictors of whether you make it through the storms—is the understanding you have going into marriage. Our perspective on marriage is profoundly shaped by our upbringing, our society, and our own expectations—and it is rarely spoken or acknowledged. But that unspoken assumption will determine whether a marriage endures and fulfills or ends in brokenness and disappointment. It is huge.

That perspective or assumption is this: Do you see marriage as a contract or a covenant? Today, even among Christians, marriage is viewed primarily as a contract, a purely social construct, an agreement we enter into with another person for mutual benefit. We may write our own vows, pledge our undying love, or express whatever terms of the contract we want to express. But contracts have conditions, and they can be very pragmatic.

Committed No Matter What, Until . . .

The typical marriage contract today, even when the terms are not spelled out (and they usually are not), says something like this: "I am absolutely committed to you, no matter what, until I am no longer fulfilled or the relationship just gets too hard for us to continue with. You meet my needs, and I'll meet yours. I will stay in love with you as long as you are responding in ways that make sense to me and make me feel loved. When you cease to fulfill me or meet the needs that

I perceive you ought to, then I have the right to tell you we have grown apart, we are falling out of love, and I can't bear to think of being this unhappy the rest of my life." That's an agreement, but it's a very conditional one.

So with multiple excuses, reinforced by a culture and a media that see marriage as disposable, many couples quit the marriage contract in one way or another. Many Christians quit not by divorcing but by living silent, parallel lives that miss the joy and intimacy God intends and, even more tragically, the beauty he wants to represent in our relationships.

A Binding Agreement

By contrast, Scripture defines marriage not as a contract but as a holy covenant. Those words may come across as strange or a little archaic; people don't think much about covenants or about anything being holy today. But if this concept becomes the bedrock of your marriage, you will weather the storms. This is what kept Theresa and me together in spite of all our baggage, all our struggles, our blended-family issues, and more. We saw marriage as a holy covenant.

> *A covenant is different from a contract because it is not just an agreement; it is a sacred promise.*

A covenant is different from a contract because it is not just an agreement; it is a sacred promise. There may be some conditions written into it—there was a lot of "if you remain faithful" language in God's covenant with Israel—but if the terms are met, it is unbreakable. It is a solemn agreement with binding force.

213

This idea of marriage as a covenant comes from the earliest pages of Genesis and is the foundation of the triangle we looked at in chapter 1. God created man and woman to be united (Gen. 2:24), and the entire relationship—one spirit, one soul, and one body—grows from that foundational truth. Male and female, joined together in a marriage covenant, grow toward God in unity with each other and with him, representing the larger picture of Christ's love for the church. As we saw in Ephesians 5, marriage is not just for the benefit of a man and woman who love each other; it reflects the direction of all of creation, God's ultimate purposes for his people.

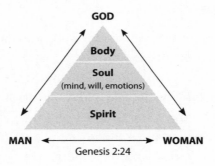

Malachi 2:14 addresses people who had strayed from God's purposes, and one of the areas of their unfaithfulness was in marriage: "The Lord is the witness between you and the wife of your youth. You have been unfaithful to her, though she is your partner, the wife of your marriage covenant." The prophet was speaking to those who were not living up to their promises, and because of their unfaithfulness, their fields were not producing crops and their enemies had the upper hand. People were wondering why God wasn't making

life work for them. The prophet's answer was that they had forsaken life's design by forsaking the marriage covenant.

A covenant is a guarantee—a binding vow. "When you make a vow to God, do not delay to fulfill it," wrote the wisest man in the world. "He has no pleasure in fools; fulfill your vow. It is better not to make a vow than to make one and not fulfill it" (Eccles. 5:4–5). When a couple stands before a minister and a congregation—"before God and these witnesses"—to make a vow about sticking with each other for better or for worse, for richer or for poorer, in sickness and in health, "until death do us part," that is very serious business to God. We may try to redefine it later. We might attribute it to the emotions we felt in that season of life before times changed. We might have a vision for how life would be better for both parties if we just went our separate ways. But none of those things were in the vow. The vow is what keeps people in the relationship when times are tough, so they can work through the difficulties and fulfill God's design for their lives.

A Promise Sealed with Blood

God established several covenants with his people throughout biblical history. The Hebrew word for covenant literally means "to cut," because it was sealed by blood—you didn't make a covenant, you cut one. The parties to an Old Testament covenant sealed their promises with a sacrifice because there is life in the blood (Lev. 17:11). It was an all-or-nothing commitment—no matter what happened, no matter who came against it, no matter how the circumstances changed, the agreement would not be violated. That is a holy covenant as Scripture presents it.

The first time we see this kind of covenant explicitly spelled out in Scripture is with Noah (Gen. 9:1–17). God judged the earth for its violence and sin, but he spared a remnant by telling Noah he would make a covenant with him. God promised never to destroy the earth with a flood again, and he gave the rainbow as a sign. There were conditions that Noah had to follow, which included worship and sacrifice.

God "cut" a covenant with Abram (whose name was later changed to Abraham) in Genesis 15 in order to establish a special relationship with him. He promised to give Abraham the land of Canaan and create a great nation from his descendants, who would be as numerous as the stars of the sky or the sand of the sea. This was unique as a unilateral covenant, a promise given by God for Abraham simply to believe. To establish the covenant, Abraham cut the prescribed sacrificial animals and waited until sunset. Normally, both parties to a covenant would pass between the halves of the sacrifices as if to say, "Breaking this covenant would be like severing our own selves." It was a symbol of how thoroughly the covenant became part of the person's identity. But in this case, God actually put Abraham to sleep and sealed the covenant himself (Gen. 15:10–17). He solemnly bound himself to his word.

A couple chapters later, the sign of remembrance was given: Abraham's descendants were to circumcise every male as a symbol of faithfulness (Gen. 17:9–14). In Exodus 34, God made another covenant with Moses and Israel, to be added to the one he had already made with Abraham. He would do wonderful, miraculous things among this nation of Abraham's descendants and establish them in the Promised Land, and they would serve God and keep his Law. The outward sign of remembrance was keeping the Sabbath.

Then in the New Testament—"testament" is another word for "covenant"—God sent his only Son, fully man and fully God, to live a perfect life among us, authenticate his ministry with powerful teachings, healings, and resurrections (above all, his own), and reveal the nature of the Father in grace and truth. And in his death on the cross—the blood of the covenant—and in his resurrection, he would save all those who believe in him so that we would not perish but have eternal life.

That's the vow. It's summarized in John 3:16, ratified in Mark 14:24, and affirmed in Hebrews 7:22, but it's really the theme of the entire New Testament. It is literally a "new covenant." And the condition that human beings must fulfill is to receive it by faith—to turn from sin and receive Christ as Savior. Jesus sealed it with his blood, we signify it by our baptism and faith, and the Holy Spirit is given as a down payment. That's the guarantee of the covenant, and God takes it very seriously.

You will find that all of these biblical covenants have four key characteristics:

- Covenants are initiated by a vow.

- Covenants include conditions.

- Covenants are ratified by blood.

- Covenants are sealed by a sign.

God's covenants nearly always include conditions. In Leviticus 26, God followed up the covenant with the consequences that would happen for those who were faithful to it and those who were not. "If you follow my decrees and are careful to obey my commands," he told them, "I will send you rain in its season, and the ground will yield its crops and the trees their fruit" (vv. 3–4). He promised to give them plenty to eat, protect them in the land, give them peace, lead them to victories over their enemies, make them fruitful, and dwell among them. "I will walk among you and be your God, and you will be my people" (v. 12). These wonderful promises were preceded by a very significant "if."

Wherever there's an "if," however, there is also the possibility of an "if not." The passage continues: "If you will not listen to me and carry out all these commands, and if you reject my decrees and abhor my laws and fail to carry out all my commands and so violate my covenant, then I will . . . bring on you sudden terror. . . . I will set my face against you so that you will be defeated by your enemies. . . . You will flee even when no one is pursuing you. . . . I will punish you for your sins seven times over" (vv. 14–18). Those are strong words, but that's the nature of a covenant. It is serious business.

Life-or-Death Consequences

God is emphatic about his purposes. He has a plan, a design for his people. He is the engineer of creation and redemption. His plan comes from a heart of love. He tells his people that he loves them, has delivered them, and wants to be with them. He wants to do life together. Now because of his love, there are some restrictions that go along with the relationship in order for it to function as it should and be as fulfilling as possible. And to discipline his people to stay within those restrictions, there are some serious consequences that come from violating them. These are not to be taken lightly. They are life-or-death kinds of consequences. Life will be really hard if his plan is not followed. But the point is that God offers his best, and we receive the best he has to offer—when we are faithful to his design. We follow his purposes, and he fulfills his promises.

> But the point is that God offers his best, and we receive the best he has to offer—when we are faithful to his design.

That was his word to Israel in the Old Testament, and it's his word to us today. Our sins are covered if we believe in Jesus and enter into his covenant of salvation, but life works only when we align ourselves with God's design. Those who remain hostile to him—whether actively in rebellion or passively by ignoring his instructions—will experience undesirable consequences. Those who embrace the grand design of the Master Engineer will find that life works as it was meant to. That doesn't mean it will be easy. It does, however, mean it will be more fulfilling.

Many Christians are wondering what went wrong with their lives. They are thinking, *But I'm a Christian! I believe in God. I have faith. I'm a follower of Jesus. Why isn't life working? Why isn't my job fulfilling? Why aren't my kids growing up right? Why is my marriage so unrewarding?* And the answer may be that they have violated God's covenant.

I am not suggesting that if you are faithful to God's covenant, then everything will work out for you. You might struggle with a job or a mate or a serious illness. We live in a fallen world, and some of God's most faithful servants have gone through extremely difficult times. What I am suggesting, though, is that if you see a pattern of all your fruitfulness being eaten up before you get to enjoy it—finances draining away, relationships stuck and stagnant, the joys and pleasures of life being overwhelmed by the constant stress of trying to make things work—you might want to consider that one possible cause is being out of line with the way God has designed you to live. If you can't figure out why you're having a lot of problems, at least consider the possibility of Malachi's message: that neglecting the covenant with your spouse can cause a sense of futility and lead to those kinds of questions.

> *Marriage vows— all covenants, actually—are a big deal to God.*

I have had several conversations with disillusioned spouses after giving this message. I remember one in particular; a woman came up to share her story about how unsatisfied she had been in her marriage. She and her husband had been married a long time, and she eventually filed for divorce. As she listened to the message, she realized she didn't have any biblical grounds for a divorce. But as she talked, I realized she was hoping for some kind of permission to go ahead with it anyway—that it probably wouldn't matter to God because he understood how difficult things had been. And as much as I would have loved to tell her that it would be okay, I couldn't. It isn't true. Marriage vows—all covenants, actually—are a big deal to God.

I don't mean to imply that if you are divorced, you are irrevocably out of line with God's will for your life. He is a restorer by nature, and he restores broken lives. The entire story of redemption is about God taking the initiative to repair us and replace the broken covenant with a new one that is entirely on him to fulfill. He is loving and forgiving, and whatever your experience with a broken marriage happens to be, you can experience that love and forgiveness completely. But God is also holy and just, and violating a covenant comes with consequences. You can be forgiven, without a doubt, but you are probably already aware that restoration is a painful process. My desire is for people to come to an awareness of the sacredness of marriage and the beauty of living according to God's blueprint. It will save you a lot of heartache.

An Irrevocable Commitment

There is hope for every marriage and for society's perceptions of marriage, but it doesn't come from presuming on God's grace, denying that there is an original design, blowing off God's standards, and imbibing the feel-good philosophies of our day. It comes from getting back to the original blueprint and honoring the One who created it. An engineer does not change his most critical specs in order to accommodate the whims of the consumer. The consumer adapts to the design. We aren't "consumers" of God, of course, but we are called to be his followers, and we cannot expect him to adapt to our changing culture. We have to conform to him.

That means embracing the true nature of the marriage relationship as a holy covenant initiated by a vow and ratified

221

by blood. When a virgin woman has sexual intercourse for the first time, the thin membrane called the hymen is penetrated and bleeds. That's serious stuff. It's the biblical picture of making a covenant and why it is described as consummating the marriage covenant. It leads to a different definition of marriage than most of us have grown up believing. While most of society treats it as a contract, God sees it as a covenant.

Marriage is an irrevocable commitment of unconditional love toward an imperfect person. It is holy, and it is permanent.

Why is this so important? Because this is an impossible task without a permanent commitment. If you go through marriage with an escape clause—knowing in the back of your mind that you can get out if it becomes too difficult—you may not press through to the end. You may get stuck in the wilderness and never make it to the promised land. The covenant functions as a glue that keeps you together through the hard times. It creates safe boundaries for each partner to be himself or herself while trying to make things work without fear of losing it all.

> *The covenant functions as a glue that keeps you together through the hard times.*

Without it, you and your mate will act not out of commitment but out of fear and insecurity, which often distort perceptions and decisions in unhealthy ways. The covenant becomes a gift, an act of grace that protects you and gives you the freedom and security to cultivate a healthy relationship. You need the certainty of the covenant to bind you together when nothing else does.

_____ Questions for Reflection and Discussion _____

1. What is the difference between a contract and a covenant? Do you think marriage is mainly viewed as a contract or a covenant today? How have your upbringing, society, and personal expectations played a role in your view of marriage?

2. Read Malachi 2:13–16. What stands out the most to you in this passage? Why?

3. Review the four key characteristics of biblical covenants described in this chapter. How are these characteristics seen in a marriage covenant? How do you respond to the idea that the marriage covenant is serious business?

4. Why is permanent commitment vital to a marriage? How have you seen this in your marriage?

5. We know that God answers prayer (Phil. 4:6–7). Will you commit to pray for your spouse and with your spouse?

16

Building a Bright Future Together

Following a common custom in Indonesia, young women who are about to get married sometimes gather together all their childhood toys and dolls and invite their girlfriends to a party to look at them one last time. Then they burn everything in a bonfire. It is a highly symbolic event that recognizes the bride's new reality: she is leaving her family and joining another one. Her old life is gone, and she is entering a new life with her husband.

Leaving, Cleaving, and Becoming One

The biblical covenant of marriage has three distinct aspects to it: leaving, cleaving, and becoming one flesh. These are based on Genesis 2:24, which spells them out: "That is why a man leaves his father and mother and is united to his wife, and they become one flesh." As the Indonesian custom illustrates, marriage involves a separation from the old and an embracing of the new. That doesn't have to involve burning old possessions or cutting off family ties, and it doesn't require you to leave town or even your old neighborhood. In biblical times, "leaving" often meant moving into another room that had been prepared for the new couple in the family home. But however far you end up from your families of origin, leaving does mean recognizing the reality of a new relationship. Old family relationships don't have to be ignored, but they do have to change. The primary relationship in a husband and wife's life is with each other.

The "leaving" implies separation. When you get married, you leave behind your dependence on former relationships, including financial and emotional strings. When you have a problem, you don't go running to Mom or Dad anymore, and you don't gossip with your friends like you might have done in high school. There's nothing wrong with getting advice from older married couples, including your parents; in fact, that's highly recommended. But they are peripheral now. They are outside counsel, not insiders. They are not your focus in sorting things out. You say to yourself and to your spouse, "This is really difficult, but I'm going to leave my attachments to them behind, and my new focus is you." That's leaving.

Then you "cleave," a word that comes from the King James translation. The best picture of cleaving is an epoxy adhesive: you are bound together. You don't just live together with your mate. You actually become one. You are no longer "you and I"; you are "us." Sometimes spouses take advantage of that reality to deny that the other person has any real individuality or personal needs, but that isn't what this means. You don't cease to be a unique individual. But you do cease to be an independent individual. Your decisions are no longer only yours. You live and move in tandem with someone else as though you are integrally connected or irrevocably joined. That is, in fact, what has happened in spiritual terms.

> *You don't cease to be a unique individual. But you do cease to be an independent individual.*

The result of cleaving is being "one flesh." If you were to mix up a pint of my blood and a pint of my wife's, it would be really hard to tell whose is whose, right? You would not be able to separate them again. That's what it means to become one flesh, and it plays out in a beautiful way when you have children, who embody the DNA each of you brought into the relationship.

In a sense, "one flesh" is an instant reality for a married couple, but living life as one flesh is a process. I had to go through counseling and read books to learn how to be one flesh with Theresa. Sometimes I've gotten stuck and have needed mentoring. When you bring all your dysfunction and baggage into a relationship with someone else who has brought all of his or hers, it isn't easy to become one flesh. It may be the biggest challenge of your life. But it comes with one of the biggest rewards you'll ever experience.

Leaving, cleaving, and becoming one are not automatic. The covenant of marriage declares some things to be true of you and your spouse; you are bound to each other as one. But experiencing oneness is another matter. A husband and wife need to be able to say to each other, "I know we have responsibilities to carry out, children to care for, money to earn, food to prepare, and bills to pay, but *regardless of whatever else is going on in life, I'm going to figure out how to get close to you.* I'm going to learn how to resolve anger, to communicate effectively, and to find some common interests and activities we can do together. Whatever we need to deal with in the meantime, we'll deal with. But whatever we need to do to make this happen, we're going to make it happen." I can almost guarantee that in eighteen months, that marriage would be radically different. And radically rewarding.

Instead, most of us want a shortcut—a quick fix. And when it doesn't happen, many people give up and either turn off on the inside or literally walk away. But quick fixes rarely have any long-term effect. Shortcuts in marriage don't work. The rewards come to those who are willing to make an effort and persevere.

The Implications of a Covenant

Because marriage is a covenant and not a contract, as we saw in the last chapter, it comes with at least four implications that fly in the face of our culture today.

1. Divorce is not an option.

We read Malachi 2:14 earlier. As we read on to verse 16, we see in the NASB and the NLT that God says he hates divorce. The verse goes on to say that the man who divorces his wife does violence to her by leaving her with no protection, no provision, and no prospects, which was especially true in ancient times. The covenant of marriage is meant to be inviolable.

I understand the nuances here. I realize there are times when divorce is unavoidable or grounded in Scripture. From the evidence in Jesus's teaching and other biblical passages, I believe there are two circumstances in which the Bible clearly allows for divorce: when a mate is unfaithful (because in that case, the covenant has already been broken) and when an unbelieving mate abandons the relationship. In fact, I married someone who had experienced that kind of abandonment. In neither case am I suggesting that reconciliation is impossible or undesirable; I've seen couples reconcile after one partner abandoned the other or had an affair, and it is a beautiful testimony to God's grace and restoration. But divorce is permitted in those cases. I would also suggest that in cases of physical or extreme emotional abuse, times of separation may be necessary.

I also understand that many people reading this book have already gotten a divorce when none of those exceptions applied. If you're one of them, you may be thinking, *I messed up, but there's nothing I can do to go back and fix things*. As I mentioned earlier, I want to be clear that even when you divorce without biblical grounds, it is not the unpardonable sin. Yes, there are consequences. But God forgives that sin just like he forgives theft, deception, and murder.

I've known plenty of men and women who have done unwise, unhealthy things and been used by God in powerful ways. The Bible itself is a book full of those kinds of people. If you read about the patriarchs' family situations, you begin to wonder how God could ever have made something good out of such a dysfunctional mess. But he did. I believe he still does that today, again and again. But if you're in a marriage now, you need to see it as a covenant in which divorce is not an option. If you leave divorce open as a possibility, you may not be able to withstand the trials, do the hard work, and eventually experience the greatest rewards of intimate union.

A covenant creates a safe arena for the kind of intimacy God wants to give you. Every human being longs for someone who can look into their eyes, see all their faults and flaws, and still love them. But because every human being is desperately insecure, we all pose and posture ourselves to hide the flaws and settle for superficial love. We act like we know more than we know and accomplish more than we can accomplish.

But superficial relationships don't feed the soul. What we really need is to be loved in spite of ourselves.

> *Every human being longs for someone who can look into their eyes, see all their faults and flaws, and still love them.*

If someone can see your baggage, your blind spots, your arrogance, your bad attitudes, and all your other imperfections and *still* accept and affirm the whole you, that's powerful. It does something for you. It is the closest experience you can have to seeing God's love in the flesh. And God designed that kind of love for marriage. But it cannot happen without openness and transparency, and no one gets that open and transparent in a relationship that isn't absolutely secure. Divorce needs to be off the table for that kind of love to flourish.

As I've said, the first five years of marriage and after the nest is empty are the two most vulnerable times in a marriage. In between, couples tend to focus on the kids—schedules, activities, schools, parenting strategies, and goals for the future. When those preoccupations are removed, many couples no longer remember how to relate to each other. They realize they have been living parallel lives all those years. It doesn't take much at that point to think about the limited time you have left and to redirect your attention somewhere else.

I remember my first really difficult and painful moment in marriage—not the first argument or problem, but the first big conflict when I questioned whether our marriage was going to succeed. We had a huge blowup, and I was hurt and angry. I slammed the door to the house, got in my car, and drove off. I thought, *Man, I can't believe how she's acting. What's wrong with her? I've married the wrong person!* At that moment, I just wanted out of the relationship. But the minute you start thinking that way, other options start coming to mind. Other people look better. You stop working at your marriage and let it fall apart.

As I was still stewing about my blowup with Theresa, God gave me a word picture. Theresa's family lived in the mountains of West Virginia, and when you walked out of their house, you'd see a rock face and hillside with a cave-like area cut out of it. There was a spring underneath this area where they had built storage for canned goods. It had a water supply and remained cool enough to store food in it.

I imagined my friend Dave, a bricklayer I had helped out some summers when I needed work, leading Theresa and me to that room. It was about 10 x 10 feet and had food, water, and (in my mind) even an exercise bike for working out. In my word picture, Dave began to fill up the doorway with blocks three feet thick. At the end, he waved, filled in the last block, and walked away. Theresa and I could eat and drink and get some exercise, but there were no TVs or books. We could go to the corner and sulk or refuse to talk for a while. But eventually in a 10 x 10 room, you have to talk. There's no way out. You can't leave until you figure some things out. So it wouldn't do me any good to spend time thinking about how insensitive she is to my needs and unaffectionate she is being, or to complain about how I don't know what to do. And it wouldn't do her any good to think the same things about me and complain about how I'm only interested in sports, my work, or anything else I get self-absorbed about.

> Quitting simply is not an option. It's a life commitment; so figure it out.

If you're stuck in the room, at some point you realize it isn't any fun, and whatever needs to happen, it had better happen. Your only resort is really to sit down and talk and resolve some things. Quitting simply is not an option. It's a life commitment; so figure it out.

That word picture became my understanding of covenant. I know I can share anything with my wife, and she can share anything with me, because neither of us is going anywhere. The relationship is not in question. The health of the relationship may go up and down over the years, but the fact of it is not going to change. We no longer look at our relationship as win-lose because if one of us loses, we both lose. It has to be win-win. And that's the context in which intimacy can really flourish because the relationship is safe.

That is why living together before marriage doesn't work. If you think there's always an escape clause, you are never really free to be yourself without worrying if it's going to offend the other person to the point of breaking the relationship. There's never complete security. So in a covenant marriage, divorce is not an option. In fact, eliminating that possibility is the key to intimacy.

2. Adultery is a serious, covenant-breaking offense.

Proverbs 2:16–19 tells us that adultery puts people on a pathway toward death. No one wins. It is a physical expression of "one flesh" with someone you have not made a one-flesh commitment with and are not involved in a one-flesh growth process with. It is a violation of what God has intended.

3. Sex before marriage is a violation of this holy covenant.

We have come across Hebrews 13:4 before, but here is the full verse: "Marriage should be honored by all, and the marriage bed kept pure, for God will judge the adulterer and all the sexually immoral." If you are sleeping with someone you are not married to, or if you are logging on to websites that encourage you to envision sexual acts with someone you are not married to, stop.

That applies long before you are married because God looks at your life as a whole, not as a sequence. If you are searching for his will for your life, this is step one. That kind of sex is not about love—it's about selfishly satisfying your own lusts. I understand why it's so compelling; it comes from a broken place inside you. And God has compassion on you and wants to heal the wounds you are trying to heal with false remedies. But that is not the way. It will not lead to healing. God will judge the adulterer and the sexually immoral.

I understand that whether this is an actual relationship or a mental habit, ending it can be really, really hard. It will play on all your insecurities and magnify your greatest weaknesses. If you are involved with someone physically and emotionally, it may cause him or her, as well as you, emotional pain. But breaking it off and changing course will be good for everyone involved. The question you have to ask yourself is what kind of marriage, now or in the future, you really want to have. If it is to look anything like God's blueprint, all the counterfeits have to end.

> *The question you have to ask yourself is what kind of marriage, now or in the future, you really want to have.*

4. Same-sex relationships are forbidden as a violation of God's design.

Holding to God's Word on same-sex relationships is a really unpopular thing in today's culture. But regardless of what apologists for alternative lifestyles would say, the Bible speaks clearly on this. "Do not be deceived: Neither the sexually immoral nor idolaters nor adulterers nor men who have sex with men nor thieves nor the greedy nor drunkards nor slanderers nor swindlers will inherit the kingdom of God" (1 Cor. 6:9–10).

Notice that God distributes his judgment fairly among heterosexual and homosexual sins—as well as among other sins that have nothing to do with sex. This is a sobering verse for everyone, not just the sexually sinful. (Whether you've ever stolen or reviled anyone, you have certainly coveted and had idols in your heart.) But it does address sexuality, and illicit sex will not only bring God's judgment but it will also undermine your own desires for intimacy. It doesn't deliver what it promises. These guardrails are given by God because he loves us. To any type of sexual activity that prevents us from experiencing the best according to the blueprint, God says, "Don't."

If you have violated these terms of the covenant or any others, the first step to restoration is always to repent. Don't let the word intimidate you; it often comes with a lot of baggage, but it simply means to turn away from the old and turn toward the new. "God, I need help" is a beautiful and effective starting point. And it's necessary because you won't be able to follow the blueprint on your own. It doesn't matter how far away you think you are from God's best; his goal is to get you there, and he will help you do it. He always gets excited about putting his people on a new path.

> *Whatever mistakes you have made in the past, the way forward is open before you, and God will walk it with you.*

Wherever you are in your journey with him, make a commitment to the path that he has laid out for you in his Word. You will never go wrong by adhering to the design. If you are in a marriage that needs some change, or even if you consider yourself to be happily married right now, make a commitment to embrace these terms of the covenant. If you are single and hoping to experience the best marriage possible, make a commitment to begin with an understanding of what the covenant means and how to live it out. Whatever mistakes you have made in the past, the way forward is open before you, and God will walk it with you.

_____ Questions for Reflection and Discussion _____

1. If God will forgive us for a broken covenant anyway, why is it important to treat the marriage covenant as a sacred, unbreakable vow?

2. For those who are married, which of the three aspects of marriage—leaving, cleaving, and becoming one flesh—has been most complete in your experience? Which needs the most work?

3. In what respects is the biblical view of marriage a countercultural statement? Why do you think there is such conflict over this issue in our culture today?

4. Are there any steps you need to take or commitments you need to make to align yourself more completely with God's design for marriage?

Conclusion

Throughout this book, we've talked a lot about biblical models and God's original design. That means, of course, that we have been looking at ideals—not unrealistic ideals, but still a template to aim for. God doesn't give us mediocre goals to match our human standards; he gives us divine goals to bring us up to his. So by nature, we have been considering things that many of us—all of us, at some point in our lives—will fall short of.

If you have read the pages of this book with a sense of frustration, a feeling that God's ideals will forever be out of reach, don't despair. I know from my own experience, my conversations and counseling sessions with numerous other men and women, and the pages of Scripture that there is plenty of grace for the journey.

God is on your side, walking with you to empower and encourage you every step of the way. I've seen him come through again and again because this life of intimate union between two people is a reflection of who he is and is always on his heart. In your efforts to align yourself with God's design for marriage, you can be confident that you are walking in his will. This is not an easy process, but it is a rewarding one. You *will* experience his blessing and favor.

In this book, we have also emphasized the "what" and the "why" about God's design for marriage and explored a lot of the "how." But no discussion of "how" can be comprehensive. I know how much of a challenge it can be to live out God's purposes in today's culture, and I know there will always be questions. Scripture is clear on God's nature, his character, and his intentions for marriage and family. It is not exactly clear on every point of how to apply his truth to your life. But by prayer, his Word, and wise counsel, he will give you the wisdom that will lead you in applying it to your situations.

Scripture is clear on God's nature, his character, and his intentions for marriage and family.

Again, know that there is grace in this process. God is not waiting for you to take a wrong step so he can harshly correct you. He gives you and your family the latitude to make decisions, even wrong ones, with every intention of getting you back on course if you have misunderstood or misapplied some aspect of his guidance. Rebellion and negligence will lead you away from him, but he will always honor honest attempts to seek his will and follow it. Keep your heart focused on him, and even your mistakes will work out for your good. He has promised to make all things work together "for the good of those who love him, who have been called according to his purpose" (Rom. 8:28). "All things" include your imperfect attempts to become the husband, wife, father, or mother he has called you to be.

If you have picked up this book on the back end of your marriage and parenting years, or somewhere later in the process than you would have preferred, you may have the tendency to think, *Wow, I should have done a lot of this, but I missed it. My kids are grown. My marriage is past its prime. It's too late.* Resist that thought. God has a way of redeeming lost and broken years for those who turn to him after the fact. I'm not sure how he does that, but he does. I've seen many people make decisions they should have made long ago and still reap the benefits of them. He is a redeemer and a restorer. He knows how to turn past mistakes into present blessings. Don't ever make the mistake of assuming it's too late for him to do that.

Finally, I would encourage you again to see this entire endeavor as a journey—not as a dichotomy of right and wrong ways to do things but as a spectrum between less biblical and more biblical, less effective and more effective, further from God's purposes and closer to them. Ultimately, we want to reach the goal of aligning as closely as possible with God's perfect design. But an either-or approach almost always ends in frustration and futility, at least at many points along the way. Your daily goal should be incremental progress.

> *Ultimately, we want to reach the goal of aligning as closely as possible with God's perfect design.*

You will probably never feel as if you have arrived, but that's okay. You may never feel as if you started early enough, but that's okay too. It's always a process, and God will bless any effort you make to move toward the destination. He will meet you at any point along the way and guide you with loving encouragement, correction, and strength. You can do this not because you are highly capable or smarter than the average person but because he says you can. Bring your willing heart to him, receive the guidance and power he gives you, and I am confident you will experience the satisfaction and fulfillment he designed you to enjoy.

Appendix

A Wife's Choice:
To Build or to Tear Down

BY DR. JULI SLATTERY

God's Word is filled with paradoxes. The weak are strong, to find your life you must lose it, the wise are foolish, and the greatest are the servants. Here's a paradox that no one seems to talk about: *a wife's greatest power is found in submission.*

I've spent the last twenty-four years striving to live out this paradox in my marriage to Mike. As a young bride, I wanted to trust God's call for me to submit to my husband's leadership. But I was also very skeptical. With a doctorate degree in psychology, why would I trust my husband's leadership in marriage and parenting? Didn't I know more than he did?

As a clinical psychologist, I also witnessed marriages in which women were minimized and even harmed because they believed they should be "submissive." I asked the Lord, "Help me make sense of your design for marriage!"

He answered with Proverbs 14:1: "The wise woman builds her house, but with her own hands the foolish one tears hers down."

Here is the revolutionary truth: every wife has power. Wives or wives-to-be, I'm speaking to you. Whether you are building or tearing down, you have power. Submission isn't about being passive but about using your power to build your home.

A Failure or a Hero

Your husband is very sensitive to failure. He secretly fears being exposed as a fraud or as incompetent. As much as he longs to be your hero, he is terrified of letting you down. Some men respond to this fear by taking a back seat. They don't make decisions or take leadership so that they don't have to risk failure. Other husbands handle their fear with bravado. They present a controlling, perhaps arrogant façade.

You, dear wife, have been given the power to frame your husband as either a failure or a hero. You are a mirror that reflects back to him either his strengths or his weaknesses—you are a reminder of his successes or of his failures. By wisely using your power can you encourage your husband to grow into the leader God designed him to be.

I have seen women develop two destructive patterns in relation to their power. Some women employ their power (even unintentionally) to gain the upper hand by dominating, manipulating, or treating him like he's another one of the kids. Often wives do this because they fear losing control or they want to avoid the vulnerability of trusting an imperfect husband. As a result, a wife's words, actions, and attitude consistently tear down her husband's confidence.

The second destructive pattern is for a woman to ignore her power in marriage—to be silent when she should speak.

Abigail or Sapphira

Submission is not weakness. It is power under control, directed toward a greater goal. Unhealthy teaching about submission in marriage has resulted in abusive, controlling, and dominating relationships. Tragically, this has contributed to the exploitation of women in our Christian culture and beyond.

Jesus was a defender of women and children. God's Word should never be used to justify or cover up abusive behavior of any kind. In a culture in which women are often viewed as sexual objects for a man's pleasure, the Christian home and church should be places in which women are highly valued, empowered, and fiercely protected.

Godly women are those who wisely use their power for great good in their homes, communities, churches, and places of work. I deeply appreciate the biblical account of a woman named Abigail recorded for us in 1 Samuel 25. She lived in a patriarchal culture, yet she was wise and judicious with her power as a woman.

Abigail had the misfortune of marrying a man named Nabal, who is described as harsh and evil. His name actually means "fool." Nabal insulted the future king, David, so greatly that David was ready to destroy Nabal and his family. Abigail wisely intervened, persuading David to show restraint. In this story, we see Abigail using her power to go against her husband's destructive and evil actions. She also uses her power to convince David to be merciful and trust in the Lord for revenge.

In contrast, in Acts 5:1–11, we witness the terrible result of a woman who did not confront her husband's evil actions but joined him in sin. Ananias and Sapphira sold a piece of property and lied to the church about what they did with the proceeds. Peter (their pastor) confronted both of them separately. When they lied, they were each struck dead by the power of God, a sobering demonstration of God's holiness.

Here's the point: God did not excuse Sapphira as a "submissive" wife following her husband into evil. We are each held accountable and called to stand up for what is right, good, and true.

Tearing Down or Building Up

Remember what Proverbs 14:1 says, "The wise woman *builds* her house" (emphasis added). This is an active role that requires discernment, wisdom, patience, and power. A weak woman isn't building anything. Due to passivity, her house may simply crumble around her. If you find yourself in an abusive marriage or church community, I urge you to reach out for help. God's design for marriage reflects Christ's relationship with the church. A Christian marriage that involves abusive behavior of any kind is a grave distortion of the Lord's will for husband and wife.

Submitting to your husband isn't ultimately about who is smarter, who has the better idea, or who was right last time. It also doesn't mean meekly obeying like a child. Submission is a conscious choice to use your power to equip and build your husband's leadership. Sometimes it means expressing your opinion or even putting your foot down. Other times it means biting your tongue or speaking words of encouragement.

God's design for marriage reflects Christ's relationship with the church. A Christian marriage that involves abusive behavior of any kind is a grave distortion of the Lord's will for husband and wife. If you find yourself in an abusive marriage or church community, I urge you to reach out for help.

Submission is a wife's conscious choice to use power to equip and build her husband's leadership. You have been given the power to frame your husband as a failure or as a hero. You have been given the power to tear down or build your home. Choose wisely!

For more information, visit authenticintimacy.com and read Dr. Juli Slattery's book *Finding the Hero in Your Husband* (Deerfield Beach, FL: Faith Communications, 2010).

Acknowledgments

Thank you, Marty and Ralph, better known as Mom and Dad, for keeping your commitment to one another when alcoholism threatened to end your marriage and fracture our family. Thank you, Dave and Polly, for showing me what a Christian marriage looks like. Thank you, Prof and Jeanne, for teaching us what God says about marriage and how to put it into practice. Thank you, Drs. Paul and Richard Meier, for the timely counseling that showed us how to repair what was broken.

Thank you, Chris and Anita, for the much needed help in turning messages into chapters; and a special thanks to Jerry for superintending the entire process and providing wise counsel as we added the final polish to the manuscript. Thank you, Charlotte, for your personal support and assistance with all the logistics.

Thank you, Chad, Mark, Erin, and Barb of the Baker Books team for helping me see the need for this book and for your excellent support all along the way.

246

Finally, this is a book about marriage, and the one person who I am most indebted to apart from the supernatural grace of the Lord Jesus Christ is my wife, Theresa.

Thank you, Theresa, for loving me, forgiving me, persevering with me, learning with me, and becoming my very best friend, my passionate lover, and my spiritual soul mate.

Notes

Chapter 1: God's Design for Marriage

1. Marist Poll, "'It's Destiny!': Most Americans Believe in Soul Mates," Marist Poll, February 10, 2011, http://maristpoll.marist.edu/210-its-destiny-most -americans-believe-in-soul-mates, accessed March 22, 2018.

2. Robert T. Michael et al., *Sex in America: A Definitive Survey* (Boston: Little, Brown, 1994).

3. Zack Carter, "Internet Infidelity: Today's Blind-Spot Threat to Marriage," PsychologyToday.com, posted June 1, 2017, accessed July 23, 2018, https://www .psychologytoday.com/us/blog/clear-communication/201706/internet-infidelity -todays-blind-spot-threat-marriage. See also Samantha Yule, "Facebook Now Crops Up in a Third of Divorce Cases over Cheating and Old Flames," Mir ror.com, posted January 20, 2015, https://www.mirror.co.uk/news/technology -science/technology/facebook-now-crops-up-third-5011205, accessed July 23, 2018:

Chapter 3: The Evolution of the American Man

1. U.S. Census Bureau, "The Majority of Children Live with Two Parents, Census Bureau Reports," news release, November 17, 2016, https://census.gov /newsroom/press-releases/2016/cb16-192.html, accessed July 23, 2018.

2. The National Institute of Justice and the Executive Office for Weed and Seed, *What Can the Federal Government Do to Decrease Crime and Revitalize Communities?* (Washington, DC: U.S. Department of Justice, 1998), 11.

3. U.S. Department of Health and Human Services, ASEP Issue Brief: Information on Poverty and Income Statistics, September 12, 2012, http://aspe.hhs.gov /hsp/12/PovertyAndIncomeEst/ib.shtml, accessed July 21, 2018.

4. Warren E. Leary, "Gloomy Report on the Health of Teen-Agers," *New York Times*, June 9, 1990.

5. James C. Dobson, *Bringing Up Boys* (Carol Stream, IL: Tyndale, 2001), 54.

6. U.S. Department of Health and Human Services, *Morehouse Report*, National Center for Children in Poverty, Bureau of the Census (Washington, D.C.). Quoted in Dobson, *Bringing Up Boys*, 55.

7. Dobson, *Bringing Up Boys*, 56. See William Pollack, *Real Boys: Rescuing Our Sons from the Myths of Boyhood* (New York: Henry Holt, 1998).

8. Dobson, *Bringing Up Boys*, 56. See Hannah Cleaverin Berlin, "Lads Night Out Can Save Your Marriage," *London Daily Express*, April 25, 2000.

9. Pierre Mornell, *Passive Men, Wild Women* (New York: Simon & Schuster, 1979), 52.

Chapter 5: The Evolution of the American Woman

1. Encyclopedia on Early Childhood Development, "Importance of Early Childhood Development," http://www.child-encyclopedia.com/importance -early-childhood-development, referencing R.E. Tremblay, M. Boivin, RDe.V Peters, eds., http://www.child-encyclopedia.com/sites/default/files/dossiers-complets/en /importance-of-early-childhood-development.pdf, updated March 2011. See also Centers for Disease Control and Prevention, "Early Brain Development and Health," https://www.cdc.gov/ncbddd/childdevelopment/early-brain-development.html; and Laurie Sue Brockway, "When Does Your Child's Personality Develop? Experts Weigh In," P&G Everyday, https://www.pgeveryday.com/family/activities /article/when-does-your-childs-personality-develop-experts-weigh-in. All accessed July 25, 2018.

2. Apollodorus, quoted in Demosthenes' *Against Neaera*, Dem. 59. Included in *Demosthenes: Selected Speeches* (Oxford: Oxford University, 2014) 11, but likely written and presented by Apollodorus during a legal dispute in fifth-century BC. See https://tinyurl.com/ycfgwfg9.

3. Gene A. Getz, *The Measure of a Man* (Grand Rapids: Revell, 2004), 35.

4. See William Barclay, *The Daily Bible Study Series: Letters to the Galatians and Ephesians* (Philadelphia, PA: The Westminster Press, 1976), 171.

5. Association of American Medical Colleges, "More Women Than Men Enrolled in U.S. Medical Schools in 2017," December 18, 2017, news release, https:// news.aamc.org/press-releases/article/applicant-enrollment-2017, accessed July 24, 2018.

6. *Profane Existence* (May/June 1992): 1, quoted in Robert H. Bork, *Slouching Towards Gomorrah: Modern Liberalism and American Decline* (New York: Regan Books, 1997), 212.

7. Christina Hoff Sommers, *Who Stole Feminism? How Women Have Betrayed Women* (New York: Simon & Schuster, 1994), 91.

8. Patricia Edmonds, "Now the word is BALANCE," *USA Today*, October 23–25, 1998, n.p.

9. "Porn in the Digital Age: New Research Reveals 10 Trends," Culture and Media, Barna Group, April 6, 2016, https://www.barna.com/research/porn-in-the -digital-age-new-research-reveals-10-trends/.

Chapter 7: Stepping Up as a Man: Provide

1. "Project on Student Debt: State by State Data 2015," The Institute for College Access & Success, ticas.org/posd/state-state-data-2015#, accessed July 24, 2018.

2. Financial Samurai, "The Average Savings Rates by Income (Wealth Class)," https://www.financialsamurai.com/the-average-savings-rates-by-income-wealth -class, accessed July 23, 2018.

Chapter 14: How to Make It through the Hard Times

1. Susan L. Brown and I-Fen Lin, "The Gray Divorce Revolution: Rising Divorce among Middle-Aged and Older Adults, 1990–2010," *Journals of Gerontology Series B: Psychological Sciences and Social Sciences*, 67(6), 731–41, doi:10.1093/ geronb/gbs089, https://scholar.harvard.edu/files/goldin/files/graydivorce_0.pdf, accessed July 24, 2018.

Chip Ingram is the teaching pastor and CEO of Living on the Edge, an international teaching and discipleship ministry. A pastor for over thirty years, Chip is the author of many books, including *Culture Shock*, *The Real Heaven*, *The Real God*, *The Invisible War*, and *Love, Sex, and Lasting Relationships*. Chip and his wife, Theresa, have four grown children and twelve grandchildren and live in California.

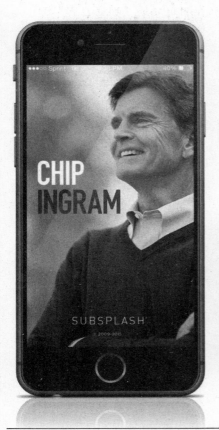

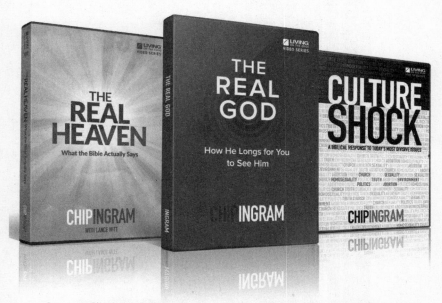

STRAIGHT ANSWERS TO
HONEST QUESTIONS

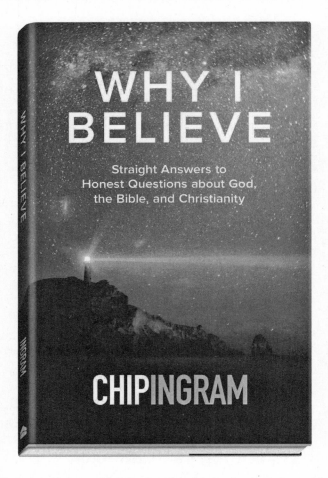

Why I Believe by Chip Ingram is a refreshing, relational approach to apologetics that explores the topics of Jesus, God, the Bible, creation, and life after death. With a heart to empower everyday believers to understand and communicate their faith with conviction, Chip offers timeless, biblical answers to the human race's ultimate questions about life and purpose.